PUFFIN BOOKS

ANIMAL KIND

All over the world animals are in distress because of human beings, yet we could not survive without them. Food shortages during and after the Second World War led to pressure on farmers to produce as much food as possible and as cheaply as possible – hence the growth of 'factory farming', where masses of animals are kept indoors in relatively small spaces. In fox-hunting, the foxes' earths are blocked up so that foxes cannot easily escape the hounds. Animals are killed to control their numbers so that they become more manageable, while other animals are kept in captivity for our entertainment and education. Even pets are not always kindly looked after – for years the tails of some breeds of dogs have been cut off simply because people think it makes the dog look better.

Is this fair? *Animal Kind* presents you with the facts on farming, vivisection, vegetarianism, pets, blood sports and other topics concerning animals. It will help you decide whether or not you want to give animals a better life, and shows you how you can do it.

Early Times is an independent newspaper for young people, which was launched in January 1988. With an estimated readership of 200,000, the paper regularly features articles on animal conservation and encourages its readers to think and act in a positive way towards all the creatures on planet Earth.

EARLY 🌳 TIMES
The independent newspaper for young people

ANIMAL KIND

Illustrated by Keith Brumpton
With cartoons by David Myers

PUFFIN BOOKS

PUFFIN BOOKS

Published by the Penguin Group
Penguin Books Ltd, 27 Wrights Lane, London W8 5TZ, England
Penguin Books USA Inc., 375 Hudson Street, New York, New York 10014, USA
Penguin Books Australia Ltd, Ringwood, Victoria, Australia
Penguin Books Canada Ltd, 10 Alcorn Avenue, Toronto, Ontario, Canada M4V 3B2
Penguin Books (NZ) Ltd, 182–190 Wairau Road, Auckland 10, New Zealand

Penguin Books Ltd, Registered Offices: Harmondsworth, Middlesex, England

First published 1991
10 9 8 7 6 5 4 3 2

Text copyright © Complete Editions, 1991
Illustrations copyright © Keith Brumpton, 1991
Cartoons copyright © David Myers, 1991
All rights reserved

Early Times would like to acknowledge the assistance of Diana Vowles in the preparation of this book.

Printed in England by Clays Ltd, St Ives plc
Filmset in 11½ pt Monophoto Sabon

Except in the United States of America, this book is sold subject
to the condition that it shall not, by way of trade or otherwise, be lent,
re-sold, hired out, or otherwise circulated without the publisher's
prior consent in any form of binding or cover other than that in
which it is published and without a similar condition including this
condition being imposed on the subsequent purchaser

CONTENTS

	Introduction	vii
1.	Wildlife	3
2.	Animals as Sport	19
3.	Health and Beauty	43
4.	Animal Farm	63
5.	Looking After Your Pet	93
6.	Could You be a Vegetarian?	117
	Useful Addresses	131
	Index	135

INTRODUCTION

Many thousands of years ago, people realized that animals could be more than just a source of meat and clothing. They domesticated the cat to keep down rats and mice, the dog to help them with their hunting, and the horse and the ox to carry their loads.

As the centuries rolled by, our demands upon animals became greater and greater. We took them from the wild and put them in cages for people to stare at. We hunted and shot them for sport. We experimented on their living bodies to gain medical knowledge. We killed birds for their feathers and big cats for their furs.

In the West, we like to think that our animals are treated very well compared with those in poorer countries. It's certainly true that in the Third World, or even in southern Europe, a half-starved animal roaming the streets or staggering under a heavy load is a common sight. But in reality, we have little to be smug about.

In less-developed countries, many people lead a bitterly hard life with not enough food to eat. Not many people who have to struggle in this way are going to lavish tender care on an animal, and certainly the animal won't be well fed when its owner isn't. And when human life is cheap, animal life is cheaper still.

So you might say that in such countries people have an excuse for cruelty to animals. But what's our excuse?

In Britain, about 2000 healthy cats and dogs are destroyed each day because they are no longer wanted. Some people don't even take them to the RSPCA or the vet to be put down – they just push them out of the car as they drive along the motorway. Or they might deliberately 'lose' them. In our inner cities, there are half a million stray dogs and 2 million stray cats – and many are unwanted Christmas presents that got turned out of their home on Boxing Day, or the victims of summer holidays when the owners didn't want to pay a kennel bill.

And it's not just our pets that we mistreat. Each year at the Grand National, horses are galloped round a racecourse with such formidable fences that deaths are common – all in the name of sport. In laboratories, animals suffer in unnecessary experiments. On our farms, many cows, pigs and hens lead miserable lives.

So we're in no position to point an accusing finger at the Third World. There's just as much animal suffering in the West. The difference is that it's less obvious – until you begin to think about it.

Many people may never visit an intensive farm, and it's certain that few of us will ever see the inside of a laboratory. But most of us have seen a Pekinese dog that snuffles and snorts all the time because its nose is so squashed up. This happens because we breed animals to fit an image we've decided is the correct one. Most of us have been to zoos and stared at the animals imprisoned behind the bars; zoos are educational, but some caged animals do suffer stress. And many of us have been guilty of wearing fur or feathers from creatures that are dying out to satisfy our desire for fashion.

All over the world, animals are in distress because of human beings – from Burmese elephants trained by terror to work in logging-camps to chimpanzees in laboratories being used to find a cure for AIDS. We have used our greater intelligence to destroy other creatures that inhabit our earth.

If this book attempted to describe all the ways in which we misuse the animal world, it would be enormous. There is only space to tackle the major subjects that affect us most – the things we can do something about.

It's all too easy to think, 'There's nothing I can do, so I'll ignore it and hope that it goes away.' The truth is that most changes are brought about by public opinion. If a small group of people call attention to something they don't like, other people will listen to them and consider the situation themselves. Some of them will agree that what is happening is unacceptable. When enough people agree, the government has to start taking notice and perhaps make new laws. As for the people who make money from animal suffering, when people turn against it, they see their profits drop and they have to find another way to earn a living.

Spreading information and altering opinion are the key ways of improving the lives of animals. Many people encourage cruelty simply by ignorance.

They might buy a brightly coloured bird in a pet-shop, not realizing that it was imported to this country in a small crate in which many died – or they might have their photographs taken with a baby chimpanzee in a Spanish resort, not knowing it was stolen from its mother in the wild and will live a short and miserable life.

We owe animals a lot. We share our planet with them, and we couldn't have survived without them. It's time to start treating them better.

I am writing on the subject of elephants. Recently lots of elephants have been killed for their tusks, which are made into jewellery and statues.

How would the killers of elephants like to be killed for their hands, feet and so on? They are ruining the wildlife and damaging God's work.

If we don't do something soon all the elephants in the world will disappear right under our noses!

I have formed a club with four girls from my class. We are raising money to get some badges and posters. We are also writing to different magazines for more members and backing. We will try to write to MPs and make the world notice.

When there is a drought or a flood most of the world helps. The elephants are disappearing and we can help as well.

Alison Ekang, aged 10,
Stockwell, London

1

WILDLIFE

All over the world, wildlife is under threat as a result of human activity. Forests are cleared, marshes are drained and roads scar the countryside. Rivers and seas are polluted with toxic chemicals, sewage and oil. Crops are sprayed with chemicals to kill pests, which in turn kill the animals that eat them.

Sometimes wildlife is destroyed through thoughtlessness. In gardens, people put out pellets to get rid of slugs, never realizing that the birds they like to feed at the bird-table will eat the poisoned slugs and die. They drain a damp ditch at the bottom of the garden and a toad loses its home. They set fire to a pile of leaves and a hibernating hedgehog roasts to death.

Sometimes it's a matter of human interests coming first. When people need food and housing, they tend not to worry very much about the loss of habitat for wildlife. If there are no laws against it, industry will get rid of its toxic waste as cheaply as possible – and if that means pouring it into the nearest river, so be it.

But worst of all, some wildlife is on the brink of extinction merely to satisfy our whims. Because some people want ivory jewellery, elephants are slaughtered in Africa. Because some people admire their coats, many species of big cats are numbered in only tens where once there were thousands. Because some people want a brightly coloured, talking bird

4 ANIMAL KIND

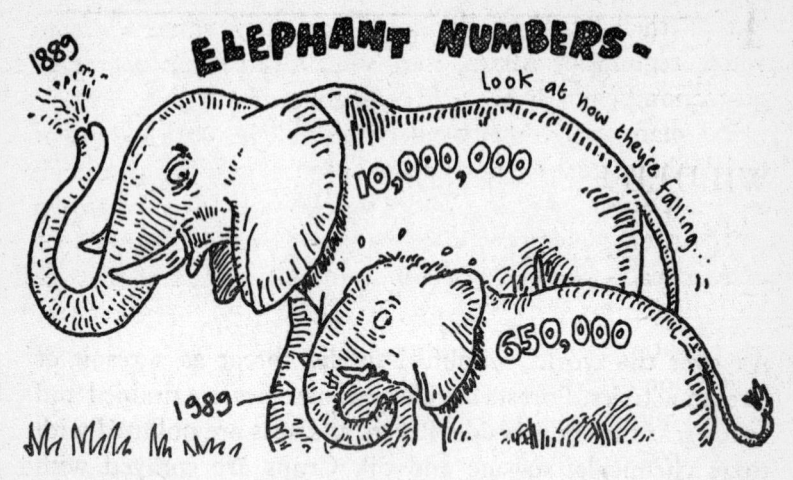

ELEPHANT NUMBERS —
1889
Look at how they're falling...
10,000,000
650,000
1989

in their living-rooms, 30 of the 329 parrot species may shortly die out.

Nearly 6000 species of mammals, birds, reptiles, amphibians, fish, insects and other invertebrates are listed as being in danger of extinction. Another 578 species are classed as 'vulnerable'. It's thought that many insects will become extinct before they are even known to scientists.

Describing all these species would be a book in itself. Here we'll examine just three animals that have caught the public imagination – the giant panda, the whale and the African elephant. They can each be seen as a symbol of all the other species that may shortly vanish into history. We'll also look at zoos and circuses.

The African elephant

In the last century there were ten million elephants in Africa. By 1970 that number had dwindled to two million. In 1989 there were just 650,000.

It's not just the ivory trade that is responsible for this. In the past, elephants were slaughtered wholesale just for sport.

But as their numbers dwindled and they vanished from whole regions of Africa, they were given some degree of protection by nearly every African government.

Yet many governments selectively kill (or 'cull') some of the elephants in their game parks because there is not enough land left to support a growing population. A fully grown elephant needs between 200 kg (440 lb) and 400 kg (881 lb) of food each day. To get this amount, it will tear off tree branches, strip off bark and sometimes uproot the whole tree to get at the top. In this way, it will destroy far more vegetation than it eats.

This might seem very wasteful, but when elephants roamed freely over the whole continent, it was a good way of encouraging new vegetation. The land had plenty of time to recover before elephants passed that way again. Now that more and more land is being cultivated, their habitat is shrinking by 2 per cent annually. This means that over 20,000 elephants lose their habitat each year.

Because of this, their numbers must be kept down in some countries or else they would starve to death. The ivory from the culled elephants and from those that die naturally can then be sold legally. This makes it hard to distinguish between legal ivory and illegal ivory that is taken by poachers.

The poachers machine-gun the elephants and hack off the tusks. Once they have killed all the older males, which have the biggest tusks, they turn to the younger males. Because elephants mature only at 30 years old, this destroys the reproductive and social patterns of the herds. It also means that the tusks are smaller and the elephants are scarcer, so the price goes up. In the last 20 years, the average tusk weight has dropped from 20 kg (44 lb) to 4.5 kg (10 lb). In the same period, the price has rocketed from around £2 a kilo to £100.

Around 40,000 elephants are killed every year. In 1988–9, only 20 per cent of the ivory that was sold was legal – and some of that had been confiscated from poachers. It's not just these poachers who are responsible for wiping out the elephants. Many of the traders must know that they are handling poached ivory. This means that the game-park rangers who are exchanging gunfire with the poachers are fighting a losing battle. As long as there are people willing to buy the ivory, the slaughter will continue.

Until 1989, the ivory was shipped to Hong Kong, Japan, Taiwan, Korea and Singapore to be carved into jewellery and ornaments. Then the EEC, the USA, Hong Kong and Japan agreed to a two-year ban on ivory trading. Unfortunately, the British government decided shortly afterwards that Hong Kong could use up its stockpile of ivory. This meant that more illegal ivory could be filtered in.

The elephant is a truly remarkable creature. Its trunk forms its nose and upper lip, and it is strong enough to uproot a tree and delicate enough to pick up a pea. Its huge ears, measuring up to 2 square metres (21 square feet), are filled with blood vessels so that they can act as a cooling device. When the elephant flaps its ears, its blood temperature drops by as much as 5°C. It lives in family herds with strong social ties – members of the herd will even try to carry an injured elephant with their tusks and trunks.

We are in danger of losing this wonderful mammal from our planet because of a combination of greed and thoughtlessness. The poachers and traders will continue the killing as long as they can make money. But if people didn't buy ivory, the trade would soon stop. It's the people who wear ivory jewellery and display ivory ornaments in their homes who are ultimately responsible for the slaughter on the African plains.

The giant panda

Many years ago, pandas were found all over China. Now there are just 1000 or so left in the mountains of the southwest.

Pandas live a solitary life in the bamboo forests. Bamboo is their main food, but because it's not very nutritious they have to eat huge quantities. In fact, they spend ten hours each day just feeding.

Their diet is the main reason for their decline. Only two types of bamboo, the fountain and umbrella, can grow in the mountain climate. Every 100 years these bamboos flower and die over large areas, leaving the pandas with no food. In the past, the pandas could move to other areas in search of more bamboos, but now they can't as so much land has been cultivated. They remain trapped in their remaining stronghold and starve to death. In the mid 1970s, hundreds of pandas disappeared in this way.

Because it's very hard to breed pandas in captivity, it's essential that they are preserved in the wild. The World Wide Fund for Nature is collaborating with Chinese scientists to monitor panda movements, and a research centre has also been set up to study captive breeding. Twelve nature reserves have been set aside by the Chinese government to prevent any further destruction of panda habitat. But because some of these reserves are cut off from one another by roads and cultivated land, the pandas are confined to small areas.

At the moment, the number of pandas in the wild seems to be stable. It is planned to link all the reserves by bamboo corridors in the hope that the pandas will be able to roam more freely. Even so, the panda remains a very vulnerable species.

The panda has never been extensively hunted for its fur. Its decline has been brought about mainly by the increase in the human population. As people need more and more land for growing food, the panda has been pushed closer and closer to extinction. It is a good example of how we must make provision for the other creatures on our planet as well as ourselves.

The whale

Whales are perhaps the most fascinating creatures on earth. Although they are aquatic, it's thought that they evolved from bear-like animals that lived on land. Even today, they still have hair, they breathe with lungs rather than with gills as fish do, and the young feed on milk from their mothers.

The blue whale is the biggest animal on our planet, weighing as much as 30 elephants or 1600 people. It's as long as three railway-carriages, and its veins are big enough for a child to crawl through. The humpback whale is the acrobat of the family, leaping far out of the water, but it is most famous for its songs, which last for 30 minutes in complicated sequences. The sperm whale hunts by a sonar-like system, making sounds that bounce off its prey back to the whale. It

WILDLIFE 9

can hear sound frequencies as high as 200 kilohertz, whereas humans can only hear up to 20 kilohertz.

These are the best-known whale species but there are several more, including the sei, Bryde's, bowhead, grey, right, fin, minke, beluga, pilot and killer whales, as well as all dolphins and porpoises. The blue, humpback, sperm, fin, sei, Bryde's, bowhead, minke, grey and right whales are known collectively as the 'great whales'.

All the great whale species have come close to extinction because of the huge international trade in whale products. In 1982, the International Whaling Commission (IWC) voted for a moratorium on all commercial whaling starting in 1985. All the 41 nations that belong to the IWC agreed to this, although Japan, Norway and the USSR continued whaling for two more years. The moratorium comes up for review in 1992.

Unfortunately, the International Convention for the Regulation of Whaling allows for the hunting of whales for scientific research. Japan and Norway have used this loophole to get round the IWC decision and are continuing to catch whales in the name of 'scientific research'. In spite of the moratorium, there is no sign that whale populations have increased.

The IWC only lays down rules for the great whales. There is no protection for the smaller ones, including dolphins and porpoises. Each year, hundreds of thousands of dolphins are killed in the process of catching tuna fish. And each year, thousands of pilot whales are killed, mainly for sport, in the Faroe Islands – Danish territory lying half-way between Norway and Iceland.

In the past, the Faroe Islands were heavily dependent on their whale catches. Nearly all the carcass was put to use. The flesh was eaten fresh or wind-dried or salted for storage. The intestines were made into buoys to float on the water. The flipper bones were used to make oarlocks and as tools to shovel ashes out of fireplaces. Skulls made good fences, and the blubber from the heads was boiled down to make industrial oil for export.

Now there is less demand for whale products. None of the head is used, because the oil from the blubber no longer has any commercial value. The kidneys and liver are not eaten because they contain high levels of mercury from the polluted sea. In fact, the islanders are recommended not to eat whale meat more than once a week because of the mercury.

As the islanders are now better off, the only part of the whale that they use is the meat from what they think are the tenderest areas. Many whales are just left to rot where they died, and many corpses float away in the sea. As for those that are butchered, much of the meat ends up on rubbish dumps because there is too much to eat or because there has been a new catch.

The islanders defend the whale killing by saying that it has gone on since the seventeenth century and pilot-whale stocks have not dwindled. But in this century, the hunting has become more efficient. Modern, motorized boats can drive the whales in from the open sea more easily. The word can be quickly spread by telephone when a herd is sighted. Two-way radios can keep the boats in touch with each other.

All this means that amateurs can join in the hunt more easily, and they take longer to kill the whales because they don't have any experience. Because the whales have a strong herding instinct, they won't easily abandon an injured member that is crying in distress. So the bay becomes full of terrified and injured whales floundering in a welter of blood.

International pressure is growing to stop this cruelty. According to the Environmental Investigation Agency, many Faroese would not even want whale meat if they had to buy it in a supermarket. The sport and the spectacle is the main reason the hunts continue.

As our oceans become more and more polluted, the whale populations are under great pressure, without our killing them too. Samples of pilot-whale blubber tested in 1985 showed the presence of two chemicals used in insecticides and some extremely toxic chemicals known as PCBs. It's thought that PCBs may affect the fertility of female whales, which means that breeding will be reduced. Environmental groups are campaigning hard to end the hunting of whales and it's hoped they will succeed – or the seas may soon be empty of these extraordinary animals.

Circuses and zoos

In the past, the only way most of us would ever see the wildlife from other countries was in circuses and zoos. We could look at pictures in books, but to see the animal itself was a novelty. And in those days, we didn't know what the animal looked like in its natural habitat. We could read how it lived, but that wasn't the same.

12 ANIMAL KIND

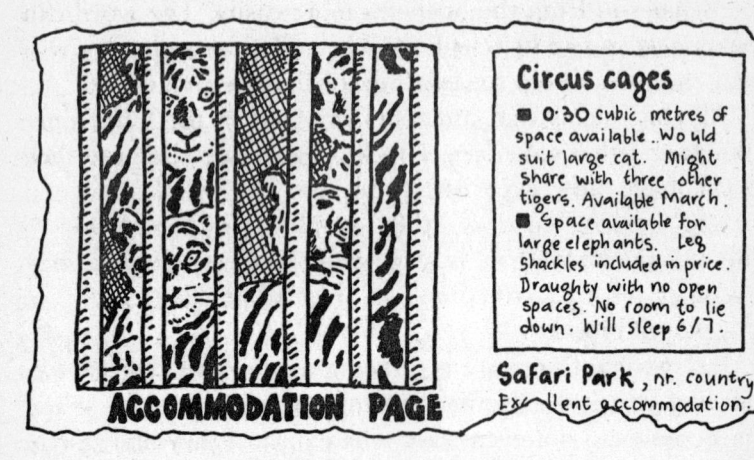

Circus cages
- 0.30 cubic metres of space available. Would suit large cat. Might share with three other tigers. Available March.
- Space available for large elephants. Leg shackles included in price. Draughty with no open spaces. No room to lie down. Will sleep 6/7.

Safari Park, nr. country. Excellent accommodation.

ACCOMMODATION PAGE

Nowadays, the television brings the wildlife of the world into our living-rooms. Superb nature films show us the animals mating, rearing young, hunting and dying in their native habitat. Many people, when they have seen a magnificent elephant in the African savannah, feel ashamed to watch one standing on its head in a circus ring. Once they have watched a tiger stalking its prey in an Indian jungle, the sight of one jumping through a hoop at the crack of the trainer's whip is uncomfortable.

For this reason, there are not many circuses in Britain these days that have performing wild animals. Some of them may just have domestic animals, such as horses and dogs. These may or may not be humanely trained, but they all live in cramped conditions and spend much of their time travelling.

In 1989 the RSPCA commissioned a survey on circus animals. This showed that many of the animals exhibited abnormal behaviour caused by stress. Elephants spent up to 25 per cent of their time behaving abnormally. Bears spent 30 per cent of their time pacing back and forth, which is a typical example of abnormal behaviour in caged animals.

The animals were found to be in very small cages. The big cats spent over 90 per cent of their lives in cages where they each had between 0.17 and 0.45 cubic metres (6 and 16 cubic feet) of space. Elephants were shackled by their fore and hindlegs for over 60 per cent of the time, and were only able to lie down with difficulty.

The report stated that in the winter 70 per cent of animals were not in peak condition and spent their whole time in buildings that were frequently not of a high quality. At one circus in Oxfordshire, 10 tigers were found in a crate only 12 × 2.5 metres (40 × 8 feet). In the wild, tigers are very territorial and they spend most of their time alone.

As for their willingness to perform, the report stated that 40 per cent of the big cats had to be encouraged into the ring by poking a broom-handle into their wagon.

It is hard to see any justification for circuses having performing animals. It's not educational to see animals doing party tricks, and circuses don't play any part in conservation; on the contrary, according to Animal Aid, 34 out of the 36 elephants in British circuses were caught in the wild. Sadly, one circus that stopped using performing animals found that its audiences dwindled – so it re-introduced them. It seems that some people still see captive, humiliated animals as entertainment.

The role of zoos is somewhat different. A well-run zoo will educate the public about its animals and will engage in conservation work. The stated aims of London Zoo are 'to increase zoological knowledge through research, applying the results to animal management, conservation and comparative medicine' and 'to increase public knowledge and respect of animals'. Over 100 scientists use London Zoo as a base for practical conservation work all over the world. Some species that are extinct in the wild have been captive-bred and returned to their native habitat.

14 ANIMAL KIND

In Kenya, the black rhino faces extinction because it is hunted for its horn. Twenty years ago there were 20,000 black rhino in the country. Now there are only 400. London Zoo has a field project in Kenya, where the rhino are safe on a privately owned ranch. Meanwhile, the Institute of Zoology at London Zoo is studying the reproductive pattern of the rhino, so that if it dies out in the wild, it can be saved from extinction by captive breeding.

These are good aspects of zoos. Unfortunately, there are bad aspects too. Many animals are taken from the wild to stock the zoos – and many of them travel in appalling conditions, which they do not survive. For example, 29 monkeys were sent from Bolivia to Japan. By the time they arrived, 15 of them had tied their tails into a giant knot, and they had to be anaesthetized while a vet took 20 minutes to undo it. Three of them were dead and three more died soon afterwards. Of 20 flamingos that were shipped from Tanzania to London, three were dead on arrival and 17 had multiple injuries to the legs and wings from tight, non-elastic straps. Out of two crates containing 1000 garter snakes, all but 78 died on the trip from Miami to London. The rest died within days of arrival.

This is the kind of suffering that can lie behind the caged animals we see. For most of them, the life they lead in zoos causes yet more suffering. They are kept in small cages where they cannot exercise properly. Sometimes sociable animals are kept in solitary confinement. Animals in the wild spend the majority of their time looking for food, but in zoos this necessity is taken away from them. A zoo animal in a small, bare cage literally goes mad with boredom and stress.

If you watch the animals in a zoo, you'll see that many of them keep on repeating the same action over and over again. It may be pacing up and down, or swinging a paw back and forth, or tossing the head repeatedly. This is a sign that the animal is mentally ill. In 1986, a survey was done on the polar bears in nine British zoos. Sixty per cent of them demonstrated this 'stereotypic behaviour', which means that 60 per cent of them were mentally ill.

The animal welfare charity Zoo Check wants zoos phased out altogether and replaced with conservation in the wild. That doesn't seem likely to happen in the near future. All we can hope for in the mean time is that public pressure improves conditions for wild animals caged in zoos.

The balance of nature

For far too long, humans have taken things from the planet without a thought. Animals have been seen solely as a source of profit, food or entertainment. Their suffering has counted for little.

Now our planet seems to be shrinking. We are worrying about the greenhouse effect, the disappearing ozone layer, the acid rain and the polluted water. We are also beginning to realize that *we* are actually dependent on the animals and plants that we once thought ourselves master of. If we exterminate one kind of animal, we find we are at the mercy of the pests that animal used to eat. If we overfish the seas, we will find ourselves short of food.

What we have to learn is a new kind of respect. Along with the animals, we are all part of the balance of nature. We alter that balance at our peril.

What *you* can do

- Contact the World Wide Fund for Nature (address on page 133). They'll send you fact sheets on conservation for a very small charge. If you can afford a subscription, even better.
- Don't buy exotic animals as pets. For every animal in the pet-shop, many will have died in transit.
- Don't buy products made of ivory, tortoiseshell, reptile skin or fur.
- Don't buy any whale products.
- Don't go to a circus that has performing animals.
- If you go to a zoo, take a careful look at how the animals behave and how they are kept. Do they have plenty of space and things to occupy them? If you're not happy with the way they look, contact Zoo Check (address on page 133). Send them as much detail as you can – how long you watched a particular animal, how often it paced up and down or showed any other abnormal behaviour. If you have a camera, send a photograph too.
- If your friends want to go to a zoo that you know is of a bad standard, ask them if they want to stare at a mentally ill animal behind bars. Once they've thought about it like that, they probably won't want to.

We should stop mistreating the world's animals. So many sports some people partake in are brutal, and make animals suffer for pleasure. We have laws against dog-fighting so we should ban fighting bulls, and as for legal snares, I would like to put a piece of metal wire round the necks of the people who set them.

As for the fox-hunters, how would they like it if they had to run all over the countryside on all fours for dogs to tear them to bits.

Everyone who agrees with me, please help. Write a letter to your local MP and MEP now.

Alan Bates, aged 10,
Crawley, Sussex

2

ANIMALS AS SPORT

The word 'sport' means different things to different people. Perhaps you might think of a tennis or football match, or school sports day. Some people think of the excitement of horse-racing, and others of the thrill of the hunt, where hounds chase an animal until they catch and kill it. Some people simply think about killing animals.

All over the world, animals are being used for one sport or another. It might be show-jumping, an internationally popular and respected sport – or it might be cockfighting, which is banned in many countries.

People disagree violently about which sports are acceptable and which are not. Bull and bear baiting, where dogs are set upon a chained animal, were banned in this country many years ago. Yet some people who think that those were very cruel sports fiercely defend deer-hunting as a fine old English tradition.

Traditions, though, need re-examining. If we stuck to all our traditions, we would still be sending small boys up chimneys to clean them, and we would still be burning witches. Just because something is a tradition doesn't necessarily mean that it's a good thing. What was acceptable to most people in Victorian times very often isn't acceptable today.

As wildlife becomes more and more threatened all over the world by environmental pressures, many people think that killing wild animals for fun is senseless. If you look at old photographs of shooting parties, you'll see groups of men standing proudly over dead lions, tigers, elephants or rhinoceroses. Not many people would find that admirable today, but to some people it's quite a different story if the animal is not an endangered species. Yet any animal with a bullet wound suffers equally whether it is an endangered species or not.

Today the animal welfare societies that oppose 'blood sports' are gaining ground. Many more people are beginning to believe that such sports are wrong, even though they are legal. But sadly, the illegal 'sports' of badger baiting and dog-fighting are meanwhile becoming more common.

Fox-hunting

Fox-hunting has been a part of the British countryside for 250 years. If you live in a town you may never have seen a real hunt, but you will almost certainly know what a hunting-scene looks like from films, calendars and Christmas cards.

People who are in favour of fox-hunting claim that it is necessary in order to keep down the fox population. They say that foxes kill lambs and chickens, so their numbers must be kept under control. They also claim that hunting is more humane than shooting, gassing or snaring because the fox is either killed outright or gets clean away. Their argument is that the people who disapprove of fox-hunting don't understand it.

The Royal Society for the Prevention of Cruelty to Animals (RSPCA) and the League Against Cruel Sports take a different view. They point out that while foxes will indeed kill chickens, very few birds are now free range. Those that are could easily be protected by an electric fence. As for lambs, only 1 out of 200 falls victim to a fox – while between 10 and 24 per cent die from hypothermia (cold), malnutrition or disease. If one particular fox is causing a problem for a farmer, it could be shot or caught in a humane trap.

Foxes are very efficient scavengers. They can often be seen in the lambing-fields, looking for dead lambs. They then carry these back to their earths (holes), and this is how they got their bad name. Shepherds finding lamb bones at their earths assumed that the foxes had killed the lambs. We now know from scientific evidence that this is not the case. In fact, the Ministry of Agriculture and Fisheries does not even keep figures on the numbers of lambs killed by foxes. It says: 'It is estimated that the loss of lambs to foxes does not constitute a loss of economic significance to the farming community nationally.'

Foxes also eat rabbits, rats, voles, insects and beetles. In this way they are of benefit to farmers, because these are pests that the farmer wants controlled. According to a National Opinion Poll survey in 1974, only 27 per cent of farmers believed that foxes were harmful to their interests. Of these, 26 per cent admitted that they based their belief on assumption rather than fact. Thirty-five per cent believed that foxes were positively beneficial because they keep rodents down.

Naturalists think that in January each year there are about 200,000 foxes in Britain. By March, these foxes will have had roughly 300,000 cubs, bringing the population to around half a million. By the end of the year, about 300,000 foxes will have been killed.

Of these, 100,000 will have been snared and another 100,000 shot. It's estimated that road accidents, natural causes and local-authority pest control will kill about 60,000 more. Approximately 24,000 will fall victim to 'terrier men' (see page 23). Fox-hunting will account for another 12,000 to 13,000 deaths.

So it's obvious that fox-hunting doesn't play a significant part in keeping numbers down. In fact, if that were the main object, different hounds would be used. Foxhounds are bred for stamina, not speed. A faster breed of dog could swiftly bring down a fox – but that would not provide much sport. As it is, hunting people hope for a good long run, where the fox gradually tires while the hounds keep on its trail. So what are the other arguments in favour of fox-hunting?

The British Field Sports Society claims that fox-hunting helps to conserve the countryside. It says that fox-hunting farmers maintain scrubland, woodland and hedgerows. In fact, it states: 'Some hunts in places where fox habitat is scarce own hundreds of acres of ground-cover in order that they know where they can find a fox on hunting-day.' This, of course, means that in these areas the foxes really are being hunted solely for sport – if there are so few that they are hard to find, they cannot be causing a problem!

The British Field Sports Society also says that foxes cannot control their own numbers and need to be kept down. The RSPCA and the League Against Cruel Sports disagree.

They point to growing evidence that in family groups of foxes only one dominant vixen (female) gives birth. If the number of foxes grows too big for the family territory, some of the cubs are driven off to find other groups. In this way a local population will always remain the same size.

So those are the arguments for and against fox-hunting. Let's take a look at what actually happens at a fox-hunt.

Hunting begins in September, with the 'cub-hunting season'. This is when the new, nine-month-old foxhounds are trained to hunt. They are taken out with older hounds so that they can learn from their example, and their quarry is the young foxes that are six months old.

By November the fox-hunting season is in full swing. The hunts meet twice or even four times a week. Before the meet, hunt followers will have gone out with spades to block up the foxes' earths, badger sets and any other hole that a fox could take refuge in.

The hunt sets out to the locality of a fox-earth and the hounds are sent in to flush out the fox. Once the fox breaks cover, the hunt is under way.

At first the fox can easily outrun the hounds. But after an hour or so, it begins to tire and eventually the hounds overrun it and kill it. Sometimes it may find a hole that has not been blocked up. Then the 'terrier men' send their terrier dogs down the hole to bait the exhausted and terrified fox until they dig it out with spades.

Foxes mate in January and the cubs are born in the spring. The fox-hunting season lasts until April or even May, so many vixens are pregnant when they are being hunted. Some have cubs that are then left to starve.

In their pursuit of the fox, the hounds will crash through private gardens, scatter cows and sheep and sometimes kill domestic animals. For this reason, many country people resent fox-hunting. Others feel that hunting is part of the social fabric of country life, so it is worth a certain amount of damage and inconvenience.

From 1972 to 1987, Gallup Polls did a series of surveys to find out what people felt about hunting. In 1972, 52 per cent of the people they questioned approved of banning fox-hunting. By 1987, that figure had risen to 68 per cent.

Yet the British Field Sports Society claims that fox-hunting is more popular than ever before. They say that some of the 200 hunts have waiting-lists for subscribers. One explanation for this might be that many people are moving out of towns to the countryside and are eager to play a part in traditional country life.

Nevertheless, the Boxing Day meet at Kenilworth Castle has been stopped by the local council. The hunt had met there for years and at the height of its popularity had many hundreds of spectators. Over recent years the numbers dwindled until finally just a handful of people turned up to watch the hunt set off. So the council, describing it as 'embarrassing', closed the event down.

It seems that Gallup Polls were getting their figures right.

Deer-hunting

There are four deer-hunts in Britain. Three of them – the Tiverton, Quantock, and Devon and Somerset Staghounds – are in the West Country. The fourth, the New Forest Buckhounds, is in Hampshire.

Autumn stags – mature male deer – are hunted from August to October. Hinds (female deer) are hunted from November to February. In March and April, the spring stags – young males – are the quarry.

The movements of the deer-herds are closely watched by a person with a great deal of local knowledge. He is called the 'harbourer'. His job is to select a suitable animal, check where it is on the morning of the hunt and report to the Hunt Master.

Because a stag does not give off a very strong scent, about a dozen of the most experienced hounds start him running. They are known as 'tufters'. After about an hour his scent becomes stronger and the rest of the pack join in the chase.

At first the stag can easily outrun the hounds. But the hounds, which are bred for stamina, stay on his scent and gradually he begins to tire. He may look for sanctuary in places the hounds cannot go, but the hunt followers will flush him out again.

Several hours and maybe 40 kilometres (25 miles) from the start, the hounds close in on the stag. He can usually keep them at bay with his antlers until the hunt followers arrive. Then he is shot.

The hinds, who do not have antlers, are often attacked by the hounds before the hunters arrive. They are often pregnant, and sometimes they may have their recently born calf with them. The calf tires more easily and can only run for about two hours before it is caught by the hounds. Hinds have less stamina than stags and they can only run for

SOMETHING FOR EVERYONE

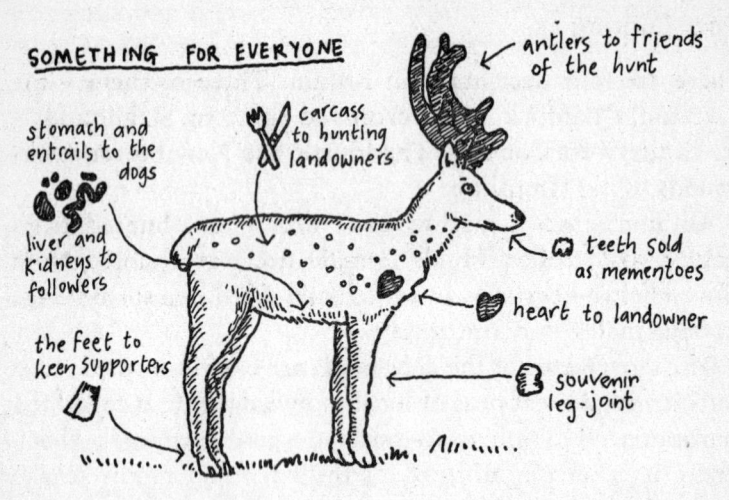

- antlers to friends of the hunt
- stomach and entrails to the dogs
- carcass to hunting landowners
- liver and kidneys to followers
- teeth sold as mementoes
- heart to landowner
- the feet to keen supporters
- souvenir leg-joint

another two hours or so before they are too exhausted to continue.

Once the deer is dead, its stomach is sliced open. The liver and kidneys are cut up and shared among the hunt followers. The heart is for the person who owns the land on which the deer is killed. The hounds are allowed to eat the stomach and entrails. The legs are skinned to the knee-joint and handed out as souvenirs, with the slots (feet) going to the keenest supporters. The large teeth are sold as mementoes. During the season, the antlers are shared between friends of the hunt and the carcasses go to hunting landowners for their dinner tables.

It's recently been discovered that even the deer that escape the hounds may die. In 1989, biologists examined a young stag that was found distressed and in pain on a Devon road where the Devon and Somerset Staghounds had been hunting earlier in the day. They found that it was suffering from acute myopathy, which has been seen in farmed deer that have been put under stress. Too much lactic acid is produced in the muscles through over-exertion and over-production of adrenalin. This causes loss of co-ordination and such pain that the deer cannot eat or drink. Inevitably, it dies.

No one disputes that the numbers of British deer must be kept under control. They don't have any natural predators in this country any more, and there are plenty of crops for them to eat.

Each year, at least 80,000 deer are shot. On Exmoor, the territory of the Devon and Somerset Staghounds, about 350 must be killed each year so that the herd contains around 1000 animals. Of these, only about 60 to 80 are killed by the hunt. The rest are shot. The marksmen pick out the old, sick and weak ones to leave a strong and healthy herd. The hunt picks out the fittest and strongest because they will supply a good day's hunting.

Supporters of stag-hunting say that farmers tolerate deer running through their crops because they enjoy the sport. Without hunting, they say, the farmers would simply shoot the deer. In fact, a National Opinion Poll in 1985 showed that only 42 per cent of farmers approve of deer-hunting. Records from game dealers show that farmers shoot deer anyway to sell the meat.

Another argument is that the red deer were nearly wiped out during two periods when there was no hunting. But these periods were between 1649 and 1660 and 1825 to 1850. Because hunting was a royal pursuit, people were sentenced to death or deportation for killing a deer – it meant there were fewer deer available for sport. When that threat was removed, people seized the chance to boost their meagre diet by killing deer. Today, deer thrive in many parts of the country where there is no hunting.

In Scotland, hunting deer with dogs is illegal. A Gallup Poll in 1987 showed that 73 per cent of people think deer-hunting should be banned throughout Britain – and only 12 per cent of the population want it to continue.

Drag-hunting

This is a much more humane way of providing the excitement of the hunt. It is popular in other European countries and is also practised in Britain.

In drag-hunting, a man is the quarry. He lays a scent trail that avoids private property, main roads, railways and fields of sheep and cattle. The hunt followers can still enjoy a good ride to hounds without causing damage or inconvenience – and there's no death at the end.

Supporters of fox- and stag-hunting claim that making these sports illegal would mean unemployment in rural areas. Yet if drag-hunting were adopted instead, the colourful pageantry and tradition could go on as before.

Hare hunting and coursing

Hares are hunted by three different breeds of hounds. There are about 82 packs of beagles, 11 packs of bassets and 24 packs of harriers in this country. Hunt supporters follow the harrier-packs on horseback but are on foot behind beagles and bassets.

The hare-hunting season is from September or October to March or April. Again, the hounds are bred for stamina rather than speed – in the view of hunt supporters, a well-bred hound is one that takes 60 to 90 minutes to bring down a hare.

At the beginning of the hunt, when the hare is fresh, it runs in large circles because it doesn't want to leave its home-range. As it tires it runs straighter and straighter until the hounds run it down. It is then killed and torn apart.

Hare-coursing is different. The season is the same, but the purpose is to race two dogs, usually greyhounds, against each other.

HARE TODAY... GONE TOMORROW

Hares are driven some distance to the coursing-field by 30 'beaters'. There a man called the 'slipper' holds the two dogs on a leash. The hare is given a head-start of about 73 metres (80 yards) before the dogs are 'slipped'. A judge then awards points to the dogs for their skill in turning the hare.

The hare may escape, but if it does not, it will be tugged back and forth between the two dogs. Supporters of hare-coursing say that it is killed instantly, but this is not so. When the handlers reach the dogs, the hare is often still alive. It is then killed, usually by having its neck broken.

There are 22 coursing clubs, although more coursing takes place outside the clubs than within them. Between 600 and 1000 hares are killed each year by organized coursing.

The hare population in this country is declining fast. The hare's diet includes many wild plants that are disappearing because of intensive farming. Toxic herbicides (weedkillers) and pesticides are probably the main culprits for the decrease in hare numbers.

Hunters, animal protectionists and naturalists all agree that the hare is becoming more and more rare. The government has spent thousands of pounds investigating the reasons for its decline. The coursing clubs sometimes even have to bring in hares especially for their events. It is hard to see any justification for killing the dwindling numbers for sport.

If the hare population recovered enough for them to cause a nuisance to farmers, they could be shot. Before 1980, around 400,000 hares were shot each year. The hound-packs killed around 6,000 and coursing accounted for another 1000. Hunting was never the main method of controlling them.

But at the moment they don't need to be controlled – conservation is what is needed before they join the long list of endangered species.

Mink-hunting

Mink-hunting takes place in summer. It's quite a new sport that has taken over from otter-hunting.

In spite of the decline in otter numbers caused by hunting and pollution of our waterways, it wasn't until 1978 that it was made illegal to kill them – although, oddly enough, it is still legal to hunt them. After the new law was passed, attention turned to the mink instead.

Early in this century, mink were imported from North America by the fur trade. They were bred all over the country for their valuable coats. After the Second World War there was a depression in the fur trade and many breeders simply set their mink free.

Like otters, mink live along river banks. The hounds criss-cross the river, checking the banks for scent, until they flush out a mink. There is a short chase before the mink takes refuge up a tree or in a hole. The hunters may destroy the tree to get at it or, if it is in a hole, it will be dug out or bolted with terriers.

Mink have a bad reputation as killers of poultry and

domestic duck. They also eat trout and pheasant that are required for sport. But they are territorial animals, and if the mink in one area are killed, the gap will swiftly be filled by other mink looking for territory. And according to the Department of Zoology at Durham University 'the mink's economic impact upon human activities is negligible when viewed alongside agricultural pests like the rabbit and brown rat.'

Conservationists oppose mink-hunting because mink often share territory with otters, which are now a seriously endangered species. There is no guarantee that the hounds will not get out of control and kill otters. Even if they do not, hunting causes a great deal of disturbance to the otters' habitat. Most naturalists believe that mink-hunting threatens the survival of our otters.

If mink numbers do have to be controlled, the animals could be shot or caught in live cages so that otters caught by mistake could be released. As with foxes and deer, hunting is not an effective method of control.

Badger-baiting

All of the sports we've looked at so far are legal. Badger-baiting and dog-fighting are not. Badgers are a protected species, which means it is illegal to kill them. Several of the people who have appeared in court charged with digging for badgers have been connected with the local fox-hunt – often as terrier men. Supporters of the legal sports put forward arguments to justify their existence. No one publicly attempts to justify badger-baiting, yet it still goes on.

A captured badger is put in a pit or chained to a stake. It is then set upon by dogs. When it is too mutilated to defend itself any longer, it is clubbed to death. Badgers have very strong jaws, so sometimes their jaws or teeth are broken so that the dogs are not so badly injured.

Another way of baiting badgers is to put them in a barrel or box. The dogs are sent in one by one to try to drag or draw the badger from the box. The dog who does this the fastest is the winner. The badger may be kept for another contest in the future.

Badger-baiting was made illegal in 1911, but it was still legal to dig for them. It wasn't possible to prove that people were digging for badgers with the intention of baiting them, so the baiting went on. In 1973, the Badgers Act made it illegal to kill, injure or dig for badgers, with an exception made for landowners who were suffering damage caused by badgers. Still the baiting continued, so a further act of parliament in 1981 made it illegal to kill, injure or dig for badgers without a licence.

But people caught digging often got off scot-free by claiming they were digging for foxes or rabbits. So finally, in 1985, an amendment to the law was made. This required people who were caught digging to prove that they were *not* after badgers. Since then, most people caught at badger sets with terriers and spades have been convicted and fined.

Dog-fighting

In the past few years, American pit-bull-terriers have been imported into Britain. These dogs are famous for their ferocity and are eagerly sought after by people who enjoy dog-fighting.

It's not only American pit-bull-terriers that are used for fighting. Staffordshire and English bull-terriers are popular too. Sometimes the American dogs are bred with the British ones to 'improve' the aggression of our own breeds.

Although they are illegal, dog-fights are well organized and run to a strict set of rules. They are held in makeshift pits, which are often carpeted to give the dogs a better

ANIMALS AS SPORT 33

PIT BULL III — DEATH OF A LEGEND
cert 'X'
produced by some very greedy breeders
directed by the owners

foothold. A fight can last for an hour or more, and it ends when one of the dogs is killed, one of the owners gives in, or one of the dogs is too frightened or injured to fight any more.

Because the owners can't take their dogs to a vet, they stitch up the animals' wounds themselves. Sometimes the dog is left to suffer for days before the owner realizes it's not going to recover and so kills it.

Training the dogs involves cruelty too. They are exercised to exhaustion to build muscle power. They are given other animals, such as cats, which have been deliberately wounded so that they develop a taste for blood. They are set against badgers to test their courage.

There's big money in dog-fighting. Champion dogs can change hands for thousands of pounds. Betting is involved and videos of the fights are sold.

It's too late to ban the importation of American pit-bull-terriers. There are already thousands of trained fighting dogs in this country. Local newspapers carry advertisements for bull-terriers that emphasize their bravery or size. Sometimes even pet bull-terriers are stolen from their owners.

The RSPCA say that they are now tackling organized crime as well as animal cruelty, and that they are dealing with a far more co-ordinated and devious group of people than ever before. They ask us, the public, to inform them immediately if we see any signs of a dog-fighting event.

Bullfighting

Most people think of bullfighting as being a Spanish sport. But a recent survey by the Spanish Ministry of Culture showed that fewer than half of the Spanish people were interested in it. In 1985 around £59 million was spent on 32 million tickets for bullfights. Much of this money came from tourists.

In most bullfighting events, six bulls are killed by three matadors. Each matador is supported by two picadors on horseback and three men on foot with capes.

A bullfight lasts about 20 minutes. The first stage is for the picadors to weaken the bull. They do this by driving lances between the bull's shoulder-blades three or four times. This damages the neck muscles so that the bull cannot toss so effectively if he manages to catch man or horse.

In the second stage, the bull is encouraged to charge at the cape. This weakens him still further because he has to make sharp turns. During this stage he is wounded again and again in the face and flanks.

The third stage is to drive metre-long spears into his shoulder-blades. The spears are barbed so that he cannot shake them loose. Each movement he makes causes the blood to run faster from his wounds.

The fourth stage is when the matador kills him.

Matadors practise killing captive cattle in slaughterhouses. Even so, only a few of them are able to kill the bull with a single thrust to the heart. If the bull is still alive after repeated sword thrusts, he is stabbed with a dagger until the spinal cord is cut.

Even then he may not be dead but just unable to move. Nevertheless, his ears and tail are cut off and thrown to the crowd.

The horses on which the picadors ride are often maimed by the bull. They are usually old and docile animals that are blindfolded before entering the ring so that they can't see how close to the bull they are being forced to go. They wear padding, but some are so badly injured that they have to be slaughtered after the fight.

Spain isn't the only country that practises bullfighting. In Mexico and much of South America it takes place in Spanish style. It's also practised in the south of France, sometimes to Spanish rules and sometimes in more humane versions. In one type, the bulls have rosettes fixed between their horns and the 'fighters' must try to grab the rosettes and escape. No horses are used in these contests and the bulls are not killed. The same applies to another style of bullfighting that is found in the Bordeaux region. Here, cows are used instead

36 ANIMAL KIND

because they are more agile and the matadors gain their points for footwork and capework.

In Portugal, no horses are used and the bulls are not killed. There was a recent attempt to introduce a law allowing Spanish-style bullfighting, but it was defeated.

Even the more humane versions of bullfighting involve distress to animals for people's amusement. To many people, Spanish bullfighting is a disgrace to humanity.

Birds

On 12 August each year (the 'Glorious Twelfth'), people turn out in their hundreds to shoot gamebirds by the thousand. This is the opening of the shooting season, and expensive restaurants stand by to get their first delivery of grouse on to the tables.

This is the date from which red grouse and ptarmigan can be shot, mainly in Scotland. The seasons for pheasant, partridge and black grouse start a little later. Closing dates for all the seasons are in late December or early spring, so that the survivors may breed to produce plenty of birds for the next season. Wildfowl (ducks, geese and so on) also have open and closed seasons when they may or may not be shot.

Pheasants and partridges are specially bred so that there are enough birds to provide a good day's shooting. For the same reason, estates in Scotland manage their grouse moors very carefully. In the 1989/90 season, there was such a glut of pheasants that one estate was rumoured to be burying the carcasses.

Because it was traditionally an upper-class sport, shooting game has a social appeal. People are prepared to pay a good deal of money for a day's shooting, so the birds represent a lot of revenue to the landowner. Unfortunately, some of the people who have the money don't have the shooting expertise. Many of the birds are wounded and have to suffer until they are picked up by a retriever and taken to the sportsmen to be dispatched.

Rooks and pigeons are classed as pests and can be shot at any time by the person whose land they are on – or by anyone who has the landowner's permission.

Boxing Day is a traditional time for hunting and shooting. All over the country, sportsmen set out with guns and dogs to shoot game. Many people who don't have the money or the social connections to shoot game will spend the day shooting rooks or pigeons instead.

The bird populations of Britain aren't only affected by our sportsmen. Many of our birds are migratory, some spending the winters as far away as Africa. On their way to their summer homes in England, many have to face the fire of sportsmen in other countries.

In spite of national and international laws, many hunters in the Mediterranean countries go out each spring and autumn to mow down the passing migrants. It's a tradition.

In Sicily, for example, the rare honey-buzzard is shot in its hundreds from carefully concealed 'hides' in the bushes and trees. It is estimated that each year no fewer than *900 million* birds are gunned down or trapped in nets. Many of them are on their way to Britain, and it's thought that we lose one in seven of our birds in this way. But the hunters think this wholesale slaughter is quite acceptable. They have always done it, so they are continuing to do it. New legislation is regarded as an interference in their way of life.

In the developed world, our birds are under threat from pollution, toxic pesticides and loss of habitat. We can ill afford to have them shot for fun.

Horse-racing

Many people think the Grand National is cruel, but in Great Britain in 1989 a total of 174 horses died in National Hunt racing, i.e. over jumps, and 26 died in flat races. That isn't the only thing about racing that is cruel. Flat-race horses are raced as two-year-olds, two years before they are mature. Carrying weight on immature spines causes deformity and pain. At the end of their racing careers, successful mares are rewarded by being sent to stud to produce a foal a year until they are too old, after which they are slaughtered. It's a tough life, being a racehorse.

Is there any good news?

As we've seen, many sports are based on tradition. They date from an age when people were even less concerned about animal welfare than they are today.

Some people enjoy these blood sports. Others don't think

about it. They'll see a hunting-scene on a greetings card and think fondly of unchanged rural England rather than thinking of the suffering of the fox.

Changing traditions is an uphill struggle. It needs people to make a stand, get publicity and try to get others to see the animals' point of view. Fortunately, some people are doing just this – but there's still a long, long way to go.

- In Portugal, the Portuguese Animal Welfare Society is campaigning vigorously against bullfighting. Their campaign against the introduction of Spanish-style bullfighting was successful, so they may be effective again.

- The League Against Cruel Sports has succeeded in buying 1012 hectares (2500 acres) of land in the West Country on which no animal may be hunted. It has 36 sanctuaries and is now the largest landowner in the region. It has also persuaded various landowners to ban hunting on over 202,350 hectares (500,000 acres) of land.

- The number of people who think hunting should be banned is steadily rising year by year.

What can *you* do?

- If you see men with spades and terriers near a place where badgers live, phone the police immediately. If you can, write down or remember car registration numbers and make notes of what the men and dogs look like.
  DO NOT approach them – some of these men may be violent.

- Join your local badger protection group. You can get details from your local Naturalists' Trust or from the League Against Cruel Sports (address on page 132).

- If you see people gathering near barns, garages, warehouses or any isolated property with bull-terriers, call the police immediately.

- DO NOT attend a bullfight.

- DO NOT buy any bullfight souvenirs – toy bulls, bullfighting posters, etc.

- If you live in the country, make sure the local hunt master knows the hunt is not allowed on your property. Even if you only have a small back garden, it's still worth doing.

- If you have a video or cassette player, tape any television or radio programmes on the protection of wildlife and send them to the League Against Cruel Sports. Many of these programmes are on local stations and it would cost the league a great deal of money to have commercial monitoring of local networks. They will copy your tape and send it back to you, or send you a new one if you prefer.

- The League Against Cruel Sports need assistance in managing their sanctuaries. If you live in the West Country or plan to take a holiday there and you think you'd like to mend fences or clear dead wood, contact them to offer your help.

'. . . No! No!' screamed the innocent rabbit as shampoo was squeezed into his eyes. A stab of pain hit him. His heart stopped with fright.

'I, I,' stammered the breath-taken mouse. All he was able to breathe in were fumes of poisonous cigarette smoke. Coughing and spluttering, he collapsed. Tears stung his panic-stricken eyes. Yet another creature was murdered.

These are just two examples of human torture and murder of innocent animals. Each day more and more animals are captured, then killed or tortured. All this for us, and our vanity.

Imagine yourself alone, away from your family with only strangers and a tall man and woman touching you and peering over your tiny body. Imagine how petrified you would be. Your heart would miss a beat whilst watching other animals being murdered and tortured.

'It'll be your turn next!' bellows an evil human.

You freeze, not daring to move a muscle. All you can feel is your heart pounding its last few beats. Footsteps. Closer and closer. They stop outside your claustrophobic cage. Then, big frightening hands squirt cream all over your delicate body. Your coat of fur is ruined and stinging. Yet still you fight it, with a pain and hurt anger staining your eyes. Something hot. Yes, you can feel heat.

'No!' you scream. You've gone in a painful way. Their experiment is complete.

For all those reading this article, I hope you have realized how many animals are treated. If you care, please buy beauty products not tested on animals or write to your local MP or a beauty-product manufacturer. Together we can work to save lives.

Clare Farmer, aged 13,
Lavenham, Suffolk

3

HEALTH AND BEAUTY

There are two animal subjects that seem to arouse more passion than any others. These are vivisection (medical experimentation on live animals) and the fur trade.

They may appear to be unrelated. But, of course, one thing they have in common is that they involve the suffering of animals. There's another connection too. Animal experimentation is also involved in the making of cosmetics. The vanity of human beings links a blinded rabbit in a British laboratory with a fox dying in a trap in Alaska.

All the animal welfare societies oppose vivisection and the fur trade. Long-established associations such as the RSPCA try to arouse public opinion against them. Some newer organizations have turned to terrorist activity such as putting incendiary bombs in fur shops or sending letter-bombs to research scientists. Other new organizations condemn violence and prefer to rely on hard-hitting propaganda.

Because the topics of vivisection and the fur trade are being fought over so violently in the media, it's sometimes hard to sort out the facts. So let's take a look at what lies behind the harrowing photographs and emotive advertisements.

Vivisection

Each year, about 3.5 million animals are used in laboratories in Britain alone. They include dogs, cats, monkeys, frogs, birds, rats, rabbits, mice and many others. Some are specially bred for laboratories. Some were once someone's pet. Others, such as chimpanzees, are taken from the wild.

The experiments include blinding, electrocuting, poisoning and scalding the animals. Over 70 per cent of them are done without any anaesthetic. Most notorious are the LD50 and LC50 tests. These code-names are short for 'Lethal Dose 50 per cent' and 'Lethal Concentration 50 per cent'. The animals are fed or injected with doses of a substance until half of them are dead. The tests last for up to 14 days. During this time, the signs of poisoning include tears, diarrhoea, vomiting, bleeding from the eyes and mouth, and crying out (which is referred to as 'unusual vocalization'). Each year, over 300,000 of these tests are carried out and the animals are not given any painkillers.

Many scientists criticize these tests as being outdated and

unreliable. In fact, there is a long list of cases where animal testing has produced unreliable results. For example:

- If penicillin had been tested on guinea pigs or hamsters, we would never have benefited from this useful drug – because it kills them.

- Morphine has a calming effect on people – but it makes cats frenzied.

- Aspirin causes birth deformities in many species including cats, dogs and rats – but not in humans.

- Thalidomide, a drug to prevent morning sickness in pregnancy, caused terrible deformities in humans – but not on the mice and rats it was tested on before it was marketed.

- The heart drug Eraldin caused serious side-effects including blindness in people – but it had caused no problems in animal experiments.

- Opren cured arthritis in laboratory rats – but when it was given to humans, there were 3500 reports of side-effects and more than 60 deaths in Britain alone.

Animals just aren't the same as human beings. Some heart drugs are tested on dogs, but a dog's heart is different from ours. Mice are usually used for testing cancers, but the types of cancer they develop are not the same as ours. This is why animal testing sometimes gives very wrong information.

Psychological (behavioural) experiments, where animals are brain-damaged, deprived of sleep, starved or separated from their mothers are even less likely to be of use to us, because animals don't behave in the same way that we do.

Many scientists still insist that animal experimentation is necessary for the sake of human health. Some point to the enormous difference that vaccines have made to the world.

Yet the British Union for the Abolition of Vivisection (BUAV) says that by the time these vaccines were invented, many of the diseases they were intended to prevent were in decline anyway. This was because of improvements in housing, nutrition and drinking-water. For example, in the 1860s, 1300 children in every million died from whooping cough. By the 1950s, when a nation-wide vaccination programme was begun, this figure had fallen to only 5 in every million. According to the BUAV, mass vaccination programmes in less-developed countries aren't effective in the long-term unless they are backed up by clean drinking-water and better sanitation, diet and housing. This means that we could help the people of the Third World far better by sending aid to improve living conditions than by selling them new drugs.

The search for new drugs is the reason for most of the experimentation. The drug companies need to make a profit, and that means making new products. But many of the new drugs for which a prescription is needed may have no advantage over those that are already available. The World Health Organization lists only about 200 drugs as essential, yet in Britain we have 18,000 licensed medicines. By contrast, in Norway there are only 1900 because a new medicine can only be brought in if there is a medical need for it.

Over-the-counter drugs – those that we can buy without a prescription – are another waste of animal suffering. Many of them don't do you any good at all – for example, none of the cold remedies will actually cure a cold, they just lessen the symptoms. Some of them are actually harmful. In Africa, where diarrhoea kills many small children, several drug companies are working hard to sell their anti-diarrhoeal medicines. One of them would not be approved for use in this country; another is only allowed in Britain for children over the age of four – in Kenya, it is advertised as safe for children over one year old. None of them is as effective as a salt and clean water solution, which prevents the dehydration that kills the children. It costs only seven pence and no animal died to discover it.

In Britain there are 442 places that are licensed for animal experiments. Most of them are owned by commercial companies. A very small number are controlled by colleges, hospitals, research charities and government departments. Altogether, 20,000 people are licensed to carry out animal experimentation.

Under the Animals (Scientific Procedures) Act of 1986, vivisectors must apply for licences for their projects. The act defines three degrees of pain that the experiments cause – mild, moderate and substantial. In 1988, the Home Office gave licences for 850 'mild' experiments, 1069 'moderate' and 44 'substantial'. But because there's nothing to tell us how many animals were used in each experiment, we don't know how many animals died in what the government considers to be 'substantial pain'.

Sadly, 'green consciousness' has led to more animal tests to check the safety of food additives and household and agricultural products. Testing for environmental pollutants has gone up by 62 per cent, and for food additives by 53 per cent. This means that many products that are appearing in the shops marked 'environmentally friendly' have been born out of animal suffering – which is hardly friendly to the environment!

Some experiments are done simply for the sake of experimentation. For example, scientists have discovered that if a cat's spinal cord is cut, the cat won't land on its feet when it is dropped. To find this out, they must have tried doing it. But why do we need to know this? What good does it do us?

In the USA, the Department of Energy funded a test on the energy of ants. Researchers made miniature treadmills

Pointless experiments Nº 1: 'Does an ant pant?'

and running tubes so that they could study the ants' breathing during forced and voluntary exercise. They found that the ants used the same amount of energy whether they chose to run or were forced to. When they were forced to run at high speed they breathed twice as fast. Most people would think that this was another unnecessary experiment.

The 1986 Animals (Scientific Procedures) Act aimed to reduce the numbers of animals that are used in experiments. So far, it doesn't seem to be succeeding. But it does at least keep some control over experimentation in this country.

In other countries, experiments are done that would not be allowed in Britain. A constant supply of animals is needed, and the export of laboratory animals from this country is big business.

In September 1989, the public was shocked when 79 beagles suffocated on a ferry bound for Sweden. A hundred of the dogs had been loaded on to a lorry in Worcestershire and were driven to Harwich, where they boarded ship. The lorry-driver and his companion left the lorry to go to the upper decks. Several people heard the dogs whimpering and complained to the crew, but nothing was done. Finally, after six hours, the driver opened the container to find that 79 had already died from suffocation and 10 were unconscious. The temperature inside the container was 35°C (95°F).

The Swedish company Astra Pharmaceuticals said that they would still use the 21 survivors for experiments. This caused a public outcry, so they changed their minds and said they would be used for breeding. Finally they announced that they would find them good homes.

Prosecutions were brought against the people responsible for sending the dogs in an unventilated lorry. But you may think that the prosecutions and the outrage seem strange — because although the dogs died a horrible death, it might have been better than what awaited them in the laboratory.

The BUAV point out that most of the important medical advances have been made without the use of animals. They say that animal testing could be replaced by population studies, clinical investigation of patients and test-tube experiments with human tissue. The RSPCA takes a different view. It says that there is no alternative to the use of animals for certain experiments, but urges the government to fund research into reducing the suffering of the animals. It strongly supports the abolition of unnecessary experimentation and points out that we could buy fewer drugs if we took more responsibility for our own health.

Population studies show how illness is linked with people's lifestyle, diet and environment. Heart disease and cancer are the major killers in the West today. Many animals die in the search for drugs to cure them.

Heart disease, which is responsible for 80 per cent of sudden deaths, increased five-fold between 1942 and 1962. We already know what causes it — smoking, overeating, food that is rich in animal fat, lack of exercise, stress. In the USA, a public-health programme made people change their diet and take up exercise. In ten years, heart disease fell by 20 per cent. It can be prevented by a change of lifestyle rather than being cured by drugs gained from animal experiments. As for cancer, the World Health Organization says that 80 per cent of cancers are related to lifestyle and environment. Yet the government spends only a very small amount of money on health education, whereas the drug companies spend millions on developing new drugs and then promoting them.

There are other powerful interests apart from the drug companies that want vivisection to continue. Many respected scientists are in favour of animal experimentation, and there are also the animal breeders and the makers of cages and equipment. It looks as if animals will have to suffer in laboratories for a long time to come.

Dissection

Animals are used for experiments in most secondary schools. Many biology and zoology courses still include the dissection of animals as part of the syllabus.

The animals that are used for dissection include frogs, rats, dogfish, gerbils, hamsters and mice. Some are supplied to the school as 'preserved specimens'. Others are killed in the schools by suffocation, drowning, carbon dioxide gas poisoning and, most commonly, a blow to the back of the neck.

Many examining boards no longer make dissection compulsory. That means it isn't essential, and there's no reason it should be – schoolchildren learn about human anatomy without cutting up humans. These days you can get excellent models and computer simulations instead.

In 1987, the Argentinian government banned dissection in schools on the grounds that 'biology is the science of life, and it is not consistent to teach it at the expense of the death of other beings; that experiments on animals are part of a dangerous process which tends to desensitize the mind to pain, suffering, to respect and to life itself.'

If the examination board used by your school demands dissection, you can ask to be examined under another board. If need be, you can seek help from the National Council for Civil Liberties (address on page 132), which has pledged support for students who refuse to perform dissections.

Testing cosmetics

The law says that medicines must be tested on animals. This isn't the case with cosmetics.

Most leading brands of cosmetics have been tested on animals. There are three main tests. One is the LD50 test that has already been described. The second is a skin test, where the animals have their backs shaved or their hair pulled out with sticky-tape. The skin is scratched and the substances are put on the skin, which often becomes sore and blistered. The third is the Draize test. In this, rabbits are held immobilized in 'stocks'. The substances are dripped into their eyes for up to seven days. Sometimes they cause swelling, ulceration or blindness, but the rabbits aren't given any painkillers.

This is the reality behind many new lipstick shades, shampoos and deodorants. When the magazines tell you that manufacturers have brought out a new autumn or spring look, you can be sure that many animals have suffered in laboratories to produce it. Many of the ingredients come from animals, too – animal glands and cells from foetuses are supposed to keep us looking young. A large number of perfumes contain substances obtained from the sex glands of civet-cats and beavers.

More and more companies are now making cosmetics that are based on plants and are not tested on animals. They are usually more expensive than the cheaper brands of standard cosmetics. This is partly because not enough people want them yet, but if demand grows, the manufacturers will be able to make larger quantities and so bring the price down. Another reason for such a price difference is that the animal products in cosmetics are often 'leftovers' from slaughterhouses that are sold very cheaply to the cosmetic houses.

Possibly because of campaigns by animal welfare groups, two of the large cosmetic houses have already announced that they have stopped testing on animals. If people buy their products because of this, the other cosmetic companies will soon take notice. Once a choice has been offered, people can demonstrate what they prefer – and no manufacturer can afford to ignore their decision.

The fur trade

As long ago as the seventeenth century, French traders were buying furs from the Canadian Indians. The Indians would bring the pelts to the banks of the St Lawrence River to supply the traders, who saw the vast forests of the new continent as a frightening wilderness.

The most fashionable fur in France at that time was beaver. As demand grew, the first official trading-post was established at Quebec in 1608. Within just a few years, parts of the Canadian waterways were empty of beavers. The Indians turned their attention to otters instead and the Frenchmen, not wanting to lose their trading partners, bought those pelts too – even though they regarded it as an inferior fur.

The Indians had discovered that fur was a valuable source of revenue. It would buy them pots and pans, guns and, most important of all, dried food that would save them from the starvation that threatened every winter. They brought furs from more and more animals to offer to the eager Frenchmen.

Since then the fur trade has grown and grown – and worldwide it's still growing. Manufacturing costs have come down so that many more people can afford a fur. In this country the fur trade is in decline, largely because of an effective campaign by Lynx, the anti-fur organization.

Today over 38 million mink and foxes are bred in farms each year. Between 25 and 30 million wild animals are trapped, mainly in the USA, Canada and the USSR. Many of them are caught by the leg-hold trap, which is outlawed in 64 countries. It was made illegal in Britain 30 years ago, yet in 1985 we imported the skins of at least two million wild animals that had been caught by leg-hold traps.

The Fur Institute of Canada says that 90 per cent of animals can now be trapped in a relatively humane way. Most of the smaller breeds can be caught in quick-killing traps. For large species such as foxes, wolves, lynx and coyotes there is no alternative to the leg-hold trap, although the Fur Institute is researching padded leg-hold traps and soft-holding leg-snares.

← first step to getting a fur coat

The traditional steel-jawed leg-hold trap has been in use for many years. As long ago as 1863, Charles Darwin gave an eyewitness account of leg-hold traps:

> I know of no sight more sorrowful than that of these unoffending animals as they are seen in the torture grip of these traps. They sit drawn up in a little heap, as if collecting all their force of endurance to support agony; some sit in a half torpid state induced by intense suffering. Most young ones are found dead after some hours of it, but others as you approach, start up, struggle violently to escape, and shriek pitiably, from terror and the pangs occasioned by their struggles.

In theory, trappers check their traplines every day. According to Lynx, the animals are often left in traps for two or three days. During this period, some of them will gnaw off their feet in an attempt to escape – although the Fur Institute of Canada claims that they only do this when the foot has gone numb. When the trapper comes to find them, he will kill them by clubbing them or standing on them.

The Fur Institute points out that many of these animals would become too numerous without trapping. They need to be controlled, and some of them also provide a valuable source of meat for the native peoples who live off the land. But sometimes the wrong animals are caught. In a coyote-trapping project in America, 1205 animals were taken. Only 138 of them were coyotes. The remaining 1067 were from 26 other species, including bobcats, golden eagles, sheep and domestic pets.

Worldwide, several species have been brought close to extinction by the fur trade. Seven types of big cat are now on a protected list and cannot be used for fur. But this means that attention has turned to several varieties of smaller cats, such as the lynx, ocelot and Geoffroy's cat. In 1984 alone, France imported 13,844 Geoffroy's cat skins from Bolivia. It's not hard to see that their numbers must be dwindling too.

The fur trade associations point out that the native people of northern Canada have few other ways to earn a living other than by selling fur. Indeed, Greenpeace has dropped its anti-fur campaign until alternative employment can be found for them. Yet Lynx say that in the 1982–3 trapping season only 200,000 animals were caught in the Yukon and the North West Territories, where most of the native people do their trapping. In the rest of Canada, four million animals were trapped. Lynx also state that in the North West Territories only five per cent of the trappers claim trapping as their full-time occupation.

Opinions are sharply divided about fur farms too. The fur trade associations say that only a contented, healthy animal will have a good coat. But the animal welfare groups point out that in the wild, each mink would have defended a territory of 4 kilometres (2½ miles) of riverbank or 9 hectares (22 acres) of marshland. Arctic foxes range over anything from 849 hectares (2100 acres) to 6070 hectares (15,000 acres). Farmed fox and mink live in small wire-mesh cages, where they sometimes turn to cannibalism or mutilate themselves.

The Fur Breeders Association approves three methods of killing mink – barbiturate injections, inhalation of carbon dioxide (car exhaust) or dislocation of their necks. Foxes are killed by attaching electrodes to their mouths and anuses and giving them an electric shock. In Scandinavia, where there are more than 11,000 fur farms, mink are also gassed with carbon dioxide.

Fur farms in this country must be licensed by the Ministry of Agriculture, Fisheries and Food and are visited by inspectors. But the Farm Animal Welfare Council, the government's own advisory body, says that UK fur farms do not meet the basic welfare needs of the animals. In one farm in Yorkshire highlighted by the *Daily Mirror*, there were dead and decaying mink in cages with live animals. About 4000 mink were crowded two or three to a cage, and the cages measured only 60 × 38 × 38 cm (24 × 15 × 15 in).

In Britain, wild foxes are snared because their pelts fetch high prices. A snare is a wire noose that tightens as the animal struggles. It will usually be around the neck, but sometimes the animal is trapped by the leg or the body. Death comes by strangulation, starvation or attack by other animals.

Snares catch animals indiscriminately. In one fox study in Wales, 4 foxes were snared – but so were 11 badgers and 1 dog. One RSPCA survey found that between September 1983 and March 1984, 86 foxes, 80 cats, 30 badgers, 18 dogs, 5 rabbits, 1 deer, 1 squirrel and 1 hedgehog were snared.

As long as people want to wear fur coats, fur-bearing animals will be farmed, snared and trapped. In no fur farm will the animals have the freedom to follow their normal

HEALTH AND BEAUTY

behaviour patterns. A British animal in a snare dies a lingering and agonizing death. Abroad there are efficient trappers who use the newest, most humane traps, inspect them regularly and kill the animals as painlessly as possible. There are also bad trappers, who leave animals suffering in leg-hold traps for days before trampling them to death. It takes up to 40 animals to make a fur coat – and there's no way of checking how they died.

Is there any good news?

- New technology is making it possible to study drug effects in cell cultures. Sometimes even small pieces from organs can be cultured and sections of tissue can be grown that give a life-like representation of a human body. This will mean more accurate testing than that done on animals.

- For the first time, the government has made funds available for research into techniques to replace animal experimentation.

- Some companies that produce cosmetics made without animal testing are finding that their turnovers are soaring. As more and more people reject animal-tested cosmetics, supermarkets and department stores are making sure they provide what people want.

- In 1987 Lynx commissioned a poll by Research Surveys of Great Britain. It was discovered that 71 per cent of people thought it was wrong to kill animals for their fur; 70 per cent wanted fur farms banned; and 74 per cent thought trapping for furs should be banned.

- All House of Fraser stores, including Harrods, have closed their fur departments due to lack of demand.

What *you* can do

It might seem as if there's nothing you can do against the might of the scientific establishment and foreign fur-trade associations. But the force of public opinion is very powerful, and you *can* make the people around you stop and think about animal exploitation.

- Join Animal Aid Youth Group (address on page 131). They'll send you a badge, poster, information pack, stickers, the magazine *Outrage* and a youth newsletter every two months. They'll also supply you with a petition asking local authorities to end dissection in schools and give you advice if your examination board demands dissection.

- Ask your head teacher if the school could view a video from the Lord Dowding Fund for Humane Research (address on page 132).

- If you buy cosmetics, choose ones which have not been

HEALTH AND BEAUTY 59

tested on animals. Beauty Without Cruelty and Body Shop are names to look for, and you will find other brands in health shops.

- Point out to your parents that household products saying 'New' or 'Improved' may have been 'improved' at the cost of animal experimentation. If in doubt, write to the companies and ask. If they say their products have been tested on animals, write a polite letter to say that you will not feel able to buy their products until they switch over to other ways of testing.

- Contact the National Anti-Vivisection Society and the British Union for the Abolition of Vivisection (addresses on pages 131 and 132) and ask for their literature. Show it to your friends, family and teachers.

- Ask your head teacher if he or she would invite someone from the National Anti-Vivisection Society to give a talk at your school.

- Ask your parents to buy organic vegetables and free-range meat as much as possible. The chemicals and drugs used in intensive farming are all tested on animals.

- When you go to the hairdressers, take a cruelty-free shampoo and conditioner with you and ask them not to use a standard product on your hair. This will encourage more people to think about animal experimentation and cosmetics.

- Contact Lynx (address on page 132) and ask them to send you their literature.

- Contact Compassion in World Farming (address on page 131) and ask for a list of anti-fur contacts and groups in your area.

- If someone you know is considering buying a fur, ask them if they know about the ways in which animals are trapped and farmed.

UPDATE

Following publication of *Animal Kind* the Imperial Cancer Research Fund wishes us to point out the following:

You should also know that thirty Nobel prizewinners, the conference of medical royal colleges and their faculties, the Association of Medical Research Charities, the Medical Research Council and 1000 leading professors have signed the British Association's declaration on animals in medical research, which states:

> 'Experiments on animals have made an important contribution to advances in medicine and surgery, which have brought major improvements in the health of human beings and animals. Continued research involving animals is essential for the conquest of many unsolved medical problems such as cancer, AIDS, other infectious diseases, and genetic, developmental, neurological and psychiatric conditions.'

A couple of days ago I watched a programme about factory farming and I think it is disgusting the way farmers treat the animals.

They put the chickens into a cage where they can only just move around and they cannot even spread their wings.

Some chickens only live for a couple of months before they get killed.

Pigs are tied down so they cannot move around very much and their piglets get taken away from them at a couple of days old.

You may think it is nice of farmers to give the animals lots of food, but they only do it to make them fat so there is more meat for us.

So if you want to stop these animals being killed, do not eat meat or if you cannot do that at least cut down by half the amount you eat.

Robert Tait, aged 10,
Yelverton, Devon

4

ANIMAL FARM

There's no doubt that farm animals have always had a hard life. There isn't any room for sentiment on a farm, and the cattle, sheep, pigs and poultry are there simply to earn a living for the farmer. The more money spent on their welfare, the less money there is to spend on the family. It's a simple equation and the animals usually come off worst.

In the past, many farmers would leave their stock ill or in pain to avoid paying to call out the vet. They'd try home remedies first, or just hope the animal would get better by itself. In those days, what the vet had to offer didn't always do much good anyway. But at least the animals were free to ramble in the fresh air and were allowed to follow their natural instincts – hens would scratch in the dust for worms and insects and cows would graze in the fields.

Today, farming has become more technological. Along with the cattle feed sales force, the Milk Marketing Board tankers and the representatives from the chemical companies, the vet is a regular visitor to the farm.

One reason for this is that the farmer feels more confident that the vet's modern medicines will work. The bill for medical attention will cost less than losing a valuable animal. But there's another reason too. Many animals today are farmed intensively. This means that as many of them as possible are squashed into small spaces. The overcrowding not only means that the animals suffer stress, but also leads to unhealthy conditions that encourage disease. If one of them becomes diseased, the infection spreads rapidly through the rest. The animals are constantly forced to the limit of their production – which means they must produce as many young, as many eggs and as much milk as possible. In fact, they must produce more than is naturally possible. Hormones and antibiotics are often used to make them grow faster, breed more and give more milk.

So life down on the farm today is often a long way away from the romantic picture many people have of it. Modern technology and modern drugs have not made life easier for the animals – and in some ways they have made it very much worse.

Let's take a look at how each type of animal lives on a modern, intensive farm.

Cattle

By nature, cattle are very sociable animals. Left free to roam in a field, they will establish a social system with family relationships and herd leaders. They divide their time between resting, grazing and chewing the cud, when they regurgitate their food before digesting it.

Dairy cows

In intensive farming, many cows are kept in 'zero-grazing systems'. This means they are kept indoors, where they can't follow their natural instinct of grazing. Grass is brought to them, and they are also given high-protein diets to improve their milk yield.

The modern cow is expected to produce ten times as much milk as her calf would have drunk. When she reaches the age of two, she is pregnant for nine months and milked for ten months every year of her life.

Not surprisingly, her life is a short one. By the age of about five years, she is worn out by the stress of overproduction and is sent to slaughter. Left to lead a natural life, she would probably have lived for twenty years.

There may be worse to come.

All healthy cattle produce a growth hormone called BST (bovine somatotropin). It controls muscle development and growth in young animals and the production of milk in adult cows. Recently scientists have found a way of producing BST by genetic engineering and the drug companies are encouraging farmers to use it.

BST increases the cow's milk yield, but the injections every fortnight can give her painful swellings. She will be more likely to develop mastitis, a painful inflammation of the udder. She will lose weight and body condition, because even more of her physical energy will be going into the production of milk. She may also lose some of her immunity to disease, and this will mean yet more drugs to cure her.

Research has been done at Bristol University into the life of the modern, high-yielding cow. From this, it has been estimated that the work she does is equivalent to a human jogging for six hours every day. BST will increase her yield still further by 10–20 per cent.

We don't actually need more milk. Under EEC rules, each farm has a milk quota and any extra milk has to be thrown away. What BST offers is the chance to get more milk from fewer cows, and this means the price of milk could come down.

If the EEC authorizes the use of BST, the large intensive farms will begin injecting their cows straightaway. This means they will be able to reduce the price of their milk and the smaller farmholders will also need to use BST so that they can compete. But because only 60 per cent of cows will give higher yields and each cow will need exactly the right amount of food, computer management will be needed. Small farms will have to become high-tech or go under.

The US Congress has estimated that if BST is authorized there, only farms with more than 50 cows will survive. In Britain it's estimated that BST would put 10 per cent of dairy farms out of business.

The drug companies say that if BST is not legalized it will be used illegally anyway, as growth hormones have been in the past. But unlike other synthetic hormones, BST can only be produced by very complex genetic-engineering plants. Only four multinational firms – Monsanto, Eli-Lilly (Elanco), Cyanamid and Upjohn – currently have the technological know-how to produce it. If BST is banned, it could easily be stopped at the production stage so there would be no black market.

BST is the first hormone created by the new techniques of genetic engineering. If it is authorized, it will open the door to many other new hormones for agricultural animals. We really don't know what they will do to our health and to the environment. But it's a safe bet that they will mean more stress for our farm animals.

Beef cattle

Some beef cattle spend most of their lives in free-range systems. But these days, more and more farmers are keeping them in semi-intensive housing.

This housing has mainly been covered yards with straw bedding. But there's a new trend now – concrete slats as flooring. More animals become lame on this type of surface, so they spend less time eating and more time lying down. Yet farmers prefer it because it saves labour.

In the USA and Australia, many cattle spend their last three months being fattened in feedlots. These are big open-air enclosures where there's no shelter from harsh weather and the ground soon turns to deep, slippery mud. Because of this, the cattle must move very slowly and carefully in case they fall. There is no grazing and they are fed instead on high-energy diets to fatten them quickly. In the UK, there is one experimental feedlot in Lincolnshire.

The life span of beef cattle is even shorter than that of dairy cows. The animals that are born in the autumn and allowed to graze are slaughtered at two years. The ones that are reared intensively go to the slaughterhouse at ten months.

More and more farmers are using the Belgian Blue breed. Because these animals have been specially bred to carry more muscle, the calves are very large. In fact, they are so large that their mothers can't give birth to them naturally. Instead they are born by a Caesarean operation.

The trip of a lifetime...

Dairy calves

When a cow gives birth, her udder at first provides a liquid called colostrum for her calf. This is extra-rich nourishment that also gives the calf immunity from disease.

The calf needs to drink this colostrum within its first 12 hours of life. It is then taken away from its mother when it is 12 to 24 hours old. For the next three days it will be given colostrum from a bucket or from an artificial teat. It will then be given milk until it is three to six weeks old, when it will be weaned on to solid food.

If the calf is a heifer (female), it may be reared to join a dairy herd. Many bull calves are reared for veal, and about a quarter of a million of them are exported to France, Belgium and Holland for this.

Many calves are sent to market at just a few days old. At the moment, there are no laws on how many times they may be presented for sale at market. This means that some face the stress of long journeys and being loaded and unloaded from the cattle-trucks many times over.

Until 1990, many veal calves in the UK were reared in veal

crate-units. These were individual stalls that were so small that the calf was soon unable even to turn round. While in the crate, they were bucket-fed a low-iron, liquid milk diet that prevented their digestive system forming properly. The crates had no bedding and because the sides were solid, the calves spent their three to five months of life in isolation. If they had not been slaughtered at that stage, they would have died soon anyway from disease caused by their unhealthy diet. When they were taken out for slaughter, many of them were unable to walk because of their diet and because they had been unable to move very much in their crates.

This suffering was inflicted to produce expensive meat known as 'white veal'. Fortunately it was made illegal in the UK in 1990, but many of the calves we export to Europe will spend their short lives in veal crate-units. Their 'white' flesh is often sent back to the UK for the catering trade.

In the UK, most veal calves are now reared under the Quantock system. In this more humane way of rearing them, they live in groups with straw bedding. They are fed with milk replacer from artificial teats. Some farmers use the Access system which is better still, because the calves have individual computerized feeding of milk replacer and dry food.

Even calves that are not being reared for the veal trade usually spend their first weeks of life in individual pens. These pens are often no larger than 1×1.5 m (3×5 ft), but at least they have straw bedding and the sides are slatted so that the calves can communicate with each other a little.

Over 170,000 calves die each year before they are three months old. The main causes of this are bad living conditions and brutal treatment at markets.

Pigs

Pigs have been called 'horizontal humans'. This is because they are intelligent, sociable animals and they are quite like us physically. Many people think of them as dirty animals, but this isn't so – if they're given good conditions to live in, they will agree on a toilet area and won't foul the rest of their living-space.

But not many pigs are lucky enough to have good living conditions. In the UK, over 50 per cent of breeding sows are kept in small individuals stalls. These stalls have metal bars and concrete or slatted floors and they don't usually have any bedding, so the sows have to lie on the hard floor.

The stalls are so cramped, the sows can't move more than one step forwards or backwards. Some of the stalls are open at the end, so the sows are tied to the floor. When they are first tethered they become very distressed and some struggle so violently that they collapse.

When the time comes for them to farrow (give birth), they are moved to another metal and concrete crate. A sow's instinct is to make a nest for her young, but again she must lie on a bare concrete floor. She stays in this crate for three weeks, suckling her piglets, and then she is taken to the boar and made pregnant again.

Her piglets are sometimes taken to wire cages that stand in tiers in darkness. When they are strong enough they are moved to concrete fattening-pens where they are crowded together without bedding. Because they would bite each other's tails out of boredom and stress, their tails are clipped. There they live in darkness until they are 24 weeks old, when they are sent for slaughter.

Tests show that if sows are fed properly and given shelter, they can produce as many piglets outdoors. The Department of Animal Husbandry at Bristol University recommends that there should be no more than 200 sows per stockman. The animals should be moved regularly to a new field so that the land doesn't get too churned up. In summer heat, sows give birth to fewer piglets but this could be solved by putting up sunshades and providing water-holes where the pigs could wallow.

Poultry

Of all the livestock on the farm, the birds probably suffer the worst. To meet the demand for cheap eggs, cheap chicken and cheap Christmas turkey, chickens and turkeys endure inhumane conditions. At the other end of the scale, geese are subjected to cruel treatment to produce pâté de foie gras for gourmet meals.

Why did the chicken cross the road?
—To get to the free range farm

Hens

The life of a battery hen is a short and brutal one. She is kept crammed in a wire cage with only a wire floor to stand on, and the floor slopes so that her eggs will roll away to be collected easily. Her wing-span is 81 cm (32 in), but she shares a cage only 46 × 50 cm (18 × 20 in) wide with four other hens.

It's not just that she can't stretch her wings. She can't perch, walk, fly, scratch the ground, dust-bathe or make a nest. These are all things her instinct tells her to do.

Under the Protection of Birds Act of 1954, it is illegal to keep a bird in a cage that is too small for it to be able to stretch its wings fully. One pet-shop owner was fined over £1000 for keeping an eagle-owl in a cage that was only three-quarters the width of the bird's wing-span. But hens are not included under the act. If the bird had been a hen, he would have been allowed to keep six more in the same cage.

A typical battery farm has about 30,000 hens, but some may have up to 100,000. Living in these cramped conditions, the hens begin to act abnormally. They become aggressive, pecking each other. They also peck at their own feathers. They suffer from hysteria and turn to cannibalism. There's a way to stop them pecking though – their beaks are cut off with a red-hot knife.

Because the hens can't get any exercise, many of them get a disease called fatty-liver syndrome. Another problem is that their bones become very fragile. A recent survey showed that a third of battery hens in Britain had their bones broken shortly before they were slaughtered. Many of those had more than one broken bone.

The hens spend a little over a year in a battery before their egg production drops. Then the whole battery is cleared out and disinfected before a new lot of hens is brought in. The 'spent hens' are sent to special slaughterhouses that deal with old hens, usually turning them into soup. They often travel long distances, 5000 of them in transport crates on a lorry. They have lived in their battery at a constant high temperature, but if they arrive at the slaughterhouse late in the afternoon, they can legally be left in the lorry until the next morning in bitter winter weather.

The European Convention for Protection of Animals Kept for Farming Purposes states that animals must be housed, fed and watered according to their behavioural and physical needs. But within the EEC, the Council of Agricultural Ministers recently reached an agreement that each hen need have no more than 450 sq cm (70 sq in) of space. This is no improvement, except in France, Italy and Greece, where the birds have had even less room. So the battery-cage system does not comply with the European Convention.

The National Farmers Union (NFU) says that because hens are now laying more eggs than ever before, they must be contented. But according to Compassion in World Farming, the hens are laying more because of research into breeding and nutrition. They say a modern chicken will lay just as much if it lives in a free-range system. The NFU also says that in a battery the hens get warmth, food, water and protection from predators.

There are 47 million egg-laying hens in Britain, and 96 per cent of them are kept in battery cages. The other 4 per cent are kept in one of these other, more humane ways.

FREE RANGE The hens live in a movable shed but can go out into open-air runs at any time of day. The organization Compassion in World Farming suggests that there should be fewer than 370 hens to each hectare (150 hens to each acre) of land, but EEC regulations allow 1000 hens per hectare (400 hens per acre). Most farmland becomes a mud-patch with this number of hens on it.

SEMI-INTENSIVE This system is not so good for the hens. They have sheds to roost in and they can go out into runs, but there can be up to 4000 hens per hectare of land (1618 hens per acre). The problem with semi-intensive egg production is that land can only be used for poultry every four or five years, otherwise intestinal disease will spread. Semi-intensive sheds cannot be moved like the free-range ones.

DEEP LITTER Here the birds live indoors. There must be no more than 7 hens per square metre (square yard). At least a third of the floor area must be covered with litter, for example, straw, wood shavings, sand or turf. There is an area where the birds can perch.

STRAWYARDS This is a better version of the deep-litter system. The birds are given plenty of space and 45 cm (18 in) of litter. Their eggs are collected and their food given by hand. Lighting and ventilation are natural, although there may be some electric light to lengthen the hours of light in winter. This system does not cost much to set up and is good for small flocks.

AVIARY SYSTEM Here there are several decks of slatted

floor perches. They are connected by ladders and there is food and water at each level. The birds are given nesting-boxes at several levels, and there are usually about 12 birds to each square metre (square yard) of floor space. Food, water, lighting and egg-collection are automated, so this system is suitable for large flocks.

PERCHERY SYSTEM This is a more intensive form of the aviary system, so it is not as humane. There may be 25 hens per square metre (square yard) of floor space. The building must be fitted with perches that allow 15 cm (6 in) of perch-space for each hen.

Spokesmen for the battery industry, and some vets, warn that there will be an explosion of disease among free-range hens. It's true that they may suffer soil-borne diseases that they wouldn't have caught in batteries – but battery hens catch other diseases caused by the way they live. Round-worms and tapeworms are also a problem with free-range hens if the same pasture is used year after year. What it boils down to is that the stockman needs to be better at his job than one who manages battery hens

Nearly all these chickens we eat – about 150 million each year – are reared intensively. They are given antibiotics that make them grow faster so that they can be slaughtered at only seven weeks old. They live in huge, windowless sheds that house up to 100,000 birds, and as they grow they have less and less space to move around in.

The floors of the sheds are covered in wood shavings, which become contaminated by their droppings. The droppings produce ammonia, which 'burns' the chickens' feet – and their breasts, too, when they rest. The sheds attract rats and flies, and sometimes the birds have maggots on open wounds.

Each year, 20 to 30 million birds die in the sheds, usually of heart attacks. A broiler-house worker described collecting the dead birds like this: 'This has to be done every day because of the heat and the way the birds are packed in so tightly. When you pick up a dead bird, it is quite common for them to be so putrid that they are just bags of bone and fluid.' Another 2.5 million birds die on the way to the slaughterhouse from injury, suffocation and shock.

It's not only the birds that suffer from this kind of intensive farming. People who live near the broiler-sites complain of pollution arising from smell, dust, bacteria, noise and traffic. Sometimes huge amounts of litter, including dead chickens, are spread on the land. One resident of Wigtoft, Lincolnshire, who lived 182 metres (600 yards) away from a broiler-site said at a planning inquiry: 'The smell itself is more than just a manure or dung smell. It is fusty and quite sickening. The smell can linger if there is no wind to blow it away properly. I sometimes have to re-do washing that has been hanging on the line because the smell gets into the clothes. My family cannot sit in the garden when the smell is present. We either go indoors or get in the car and drive away from the village.'

Pegging out the washing

Turkeys

Nearly all turkeys are reared in the same way as broiler chickens – in their thousands in huge sheds. Like chickens, they suffer from ammonia burns from the contaminated litter they stand in. The tips of their beaks are cut off, because in these overcrowded conditions they may turn cannibal. They spend three to five months of life in these sheds before they are slaughtered.

Geese

Since Roman times, farmers in France have force-fed geese to make their livers grow extra large. The liver is then used to make a special pâté called pâté de foie gras.

Until the geese are four months old they are reared free-range on grass. Then they are kept in a box so that they cannot exercise and are force-fed for three to four weeks.

Traditionally, the grandmother of the family has always had the job of feeding the geese. She kneels astride them and pushes a funnel down their throats. Then she pours warm cooked mash down the funnel and packs it down with a wooden pusher. The geese are forced to eat far more than they would normally, so their bodies and livers swell. During the force-feeding period their weight increases by 61 per cent, but their livers increase by 371 per cent.

As their livers swell, the geese find it harder and harder to breathe. They are bled to death on the farm because they would not survive being transported to slaughterhouses.

It takes five hours to feed 60 geese in this way, so a modern, faster method has been found. The bird is put into a brace that holds its wings tight against its body and stretches its neck. Its head is raised so that the funnel tube goes into its throat and another brace is put at the back of the head so it

MENU OF THE DAY

cannot move or close its throat. The person feeding the goose has a foot pedal to push the maize down the funnel, so that he or she has both hands free to massage the food down the bird's throat. On some farms, an elastic band is put around the bird's throat so that it cannot retch up the food.

The geese are given 600 g (1¼lb) of maize a day in the first week, 1000 g (2¼lb) in the second week and up to 3000 g (6½lb) a day before slaughter. This is the equivalent of a person eating 12.75 kg (28 lb) of spaghetti a day.

Sheep

So far, sheep have not been intensively farmed, although people are experimenting with ways to do this. But they have not escaped the modern method of giving animals hormones and antibiotics to control their growth and breeding.

Until recently, twin lambs weren't a common sight. Now a farmer expects twin lambs from most of his hormone-treated ewes and some are born in January instead of spring, when the weather is milder. This is so that people can be eating 'spring lamb' by Easter.

In this country, many lambs have their tails clipped to keep their rear ends cleaner. This is because flies lay eggs in the wool around the sheep's rectum ('flystrike') and the eggs hatch into maggots that burrow into the skin to eat the flesh. Clipping tails does reduce flystrike, but it is done without any anaesthetic. Fortunately, more and more farmers are fixing a special rubber ring to the tail. This cuts off the blood supply so that the tail eventually drops off without leaving a wound.

In Australia, vast herds of sheep roam with no one to take proper care of them. To prevent flystrike, the stockmen use a technique they call 'mulesing'. This means cutting away the skin around the tail of each lamb so that wool will never grow there again, even when the raw flesh has healed over. Again, this is done without anaesthetic. If the sheep were kept in smaller herds with more stockmen to look after them, it would not be necessary – flystrike could be kept at bay by trimming the wool and spraying with insecticide.

Frogs

Frogs' legs have always been a popular dish in France. Now you can get them in more and more British restaurants.

Most of the frogs' legs imported into Britain come from Indonesia and Bangladesh, where 300 million wild frogs are caught and killed each year. They are packed 300 to a sack and transported, often for several days, to freezer factories. Between 20 and 50 per cent of the frogs die in these bags.

At the factories, the live frogs are still conscious as they are thrust against a curved blade that cuts them in two. Because amphibians take a long time to die, the top half of the frog can live for another hour.

This doesn't just inflict suffering on the frogs. Killing so many of them also causes environmental damage. Frogs live on waterborne pests that destroy crops and carry dangerous diseases such as malaria. Because the frogs are being killed in huge quantities, the pests are multiplying and people are at risk. At the peak of the Indian frog trade, India was earning £5.5 million in foreign exchange from exporting frogs' legs – but had to spend £13 million importing poisonous chemicals to kill the pests the frogs would have eaten. India has now banned the killing of frogs.

In Taiwan and Brazil, frog-breeding farms are the new trend. Tests have shown that 14 per cent of frogs from these farms carry typhoid. In Indonesia and Bangladesh, the freezer factories are often unhygienic and the frogs' legs are packed in ice made from unclean water.

Do you want to eat frogs' legs?

Deer

Until recently, venison (deer's meat) was expensive and you

could only find it at certain times of the year. This was because it all came from wild deer, which could only be killed in the shooting season. Like other meat that comes from wild animals, venison was classed as 'game'. Now deer farms are becoming more and more common. Venison is on every restaurant menu, and you can even get 'veniburgers'.

Farmed deer are kept free-range in herds. The problem is the way they are slaughtered.

Deer are not domestic animals. Unlike sheep, pigs and cows, which have been domesticated for thousands of years, they are not used to being handled. Even the domestic animals are terrified in the markets and slaughterhouses, but the stress is much worse for a wild animal.

At the moment most deer are shot in the field while they are grazing, which is the most humane way of killing them. But the meat industry and the abattoirs are keen to develop the venison industry. Transporting the deer to slaughterhouses is a much quicker way of getting them on to the table.

At present deer are protected by the 1911 Protection of Animals Act. This makes it illegal to terrify or cause unnecessary suffering to an animal in captivity. This means that a farmer sending deer to market could be sued because, as they are wild animals, they would certainly be terrified.

An act of parliament that laid down rules as to how deer must be handled and killed in slaughterhouses was recently brought before the House of Commons. This would have included them under the same act as cattle, sheep, pigs and poultry and would have lessened their protection under the 1911 act. Compassion in World Farming campaigned vigorously against this and the act was defeated. At the time, the *Meat Trades Journal* said: 'The developing venison industry has been dealt a severe blow.' The meat industry will continue to lobby for abattoir slaughter for deer. It is up to us, the consumers, to make our views known if we don't think the abattoir slaughter of deer is right.

To the slaughterhouse

In the last ten years, the number of slaughterhouses has been halved. The small local slaughterhouses have closed down and this means the animals must travel long distances. Many animals are sent to the slaughterhouse because they are injured. They fetch a better price alive than if they are slaughtered on the farm. In fact, the abattoir will only accept a dead animal if it has been given a veterinary certificate, which costs the farmer more money. For these live animals, the long journey adds to their suffering.

Many more animals are injured between the farm and the abattoir. This may be because of rough handling at the markets, or because they have fallen in the cattle-trucks.

Once at the abattoir, the animals may be kept for some time in a waiting area. Sometimes they don't have any water to drink. They are already suffering stress because of the journey, the strange surroundings and the noise.

EEC and UK regulations state that animals must be stunned before they are killed. Yet, in spite of this, it is estimated that 90 per cent of animals worldwide are conscious when they are slaughtered. Many of them are slaughtered in this country.

There are several methods of stunning. Some of them are based on giving the animal an electric shock. Otherwise, a bolt is fired at the animal's head to make it unconscious.

All these methods should work. They very often don't because they are not applied correctly. For example, if the bolt is not aimed at the right place or the animal moves its head, it may still be conscious when it is killed. With the electrical methods, tongs with electrodes should be held against the animal's head for a certain number of seconds. Very often they are applied for only half that time.

The British Veterinary Association is demanding an official training scheme for slaughterhouse staff. It wants all staff to have a certificate to show that they have been trained and higher penalties for breaking regulations (at the moment, the maximum fine is only £400). It also wants a ruling that the animal must be restrained while it is being stunned to prevent so many mistakes.

Until recently, it was believed that the animal would not 'bleed out' properly unless its heart was still beating when it was killed. But tests have now shown that it doesn't make any difference. This means that a more effective and humane type of stunning, called 'head-to-back electrical stunning', may be the future way of slaughtering. With this method, the animal dies from heart failure only 30 seconds after it has been stunned.

In this country, an exception to the law is made for animals killed for Jewish and Muslim communities. They are slaughtered while still conscious by a person of either of these faiths, who has a special licence to do this. The British Veterinary Association and the Farm Animal Welfare Council are putting pressure on the government to end this. They say that the animal must feel pain before it becomes unconscious from lack of blood. So far, our government has refused to ban this ritual slaughter because it does not want to interfere with religious beliefs. But in Norway, Sweden and Switzerland it is banned.

Once the animal has been stunned, it is moved by a conveyor to the bleeding area where it is 'stuck' (has its throat cut). It is important that the right cut is made so that the blood flows fast and the animal dies quickly.

Sometimes the meat is made more tender by electrically stimulating the flesh before the animal is 'stuck'. The animal may recover consciousness while this is happening. Another way of tenderizing meat is to give the animal an injection of papain enzyme into the jugular vein 20 minutes before it is slaughtered. The British Veterinary Association wants this banned as the animals sometimes collapse from shock.

Poultry are slaughtered in a different way. They are hung upside down on a moving conveyor belt. The law says that turkeys may be hung upside down for six minutes, chickens for three. The conveyor belt takes them to an electrified water-bath, or stunner. When their heads are dipped in the water they should become unconscious.

From the stunner, the conveyor belt takes them on to an automatic knife, which cuts their throats. Then they are taken on to the scalding-tank.

Unfortunately, several things can go wrong during this process. Some birds lift their heads so that they don't go into the water-bath. This means that they are conscious when they reach the automatic knife. And if the knife is not set correctly, they enter the scalding-tank alive

The law now makes it compulsory for the knife to be manually adjusted at frequent intervals. But it is still estimated that as many as 10 to 15 per cent of birds are only injured by the knife.

The manufacturers of poultry-killing-systems do not even claim they are 100 per cent efficient. One automatic turkey-killer is advertised as having an efficiency rate of 94 to 96 per cent. This means that an average of 237 birds each hour are not humanely killed.

In 1984 the Farm Animal Welfare Council, which is the government's own advisory body, made 117 recommendations. Many of these were to ensure proper licensing of slaughterhouses and training of staff. They also called for the presence of a welfare official at each slaughterhouse, and an end to the piece-rate system. Under this system, the staff are paid for the number of animals they kill. Slaughterhouse staff are not well paid, so they may be tempted to skimp on stunning methods to save time.

Yet the government ignored most of the recommendations, including that of ending the piece-rate system. They say that this is a matter for the slaughterhouse-owner to decide.

It's obvious that there's a lot wrong in our slaughterhouses. Yet, in some ways, the animals that are slaughtered in this country are the lucky ones.

Each year, we export millions of animals for slaughter abroad. Ten thousand animals each week are put aboard ship in Dover alone. They then face gruelling journeys when they reach the other side of the Channel. Sheep suffer the worst, because they travel in multi-deck lorries. Often the top-deck is uncovered, which means they sometimes jump off. They may be injured by overhanging branches, and they travel long distances in bad weather conditions.

The law states that the animals must be rested every 12 hours. But this frequently doesn't happen. RSPCA officials sometimes follow the lorries on their long journeys and report frequent abuse. For example, they tracked one lorry-load of veal calves to the south of France. The calves had not been fed for 26 hours.

The south of France is a frequent destination for our animals – 2000 sheep a week go to just one of the farms there. It is believed that many of them are reloaded on to trucks and sent to Spain, where the conditions in the slaughterhouses are not acceptable in this country.

Some animals must travel even further. Sheep are sent as far as Turkey, Greece, Sicily and North Africa.

After 1992 many of Britain's horses, ponies and donkeys may be shipped abroad for slaughter, because of changes in legislation. Horse-lovers fear that this may encourage people to breed them specially for meat.

Some animal welfare societies think that the export of live animals for slaughter should be stopped altogether. But the government says that it is not right for farmers to lose money from export trade while animals still travel between other countries in the EEC.

During the Second World War, meat was rationed. Because each person was only allowed a very small amount each week, many slaughterhouses closed down.

Sunday roast, war-time style.

Since the war, many new laws have been introduced to make the slaughtering of animals more humane. Yet we still have a long way to go. Some slaughterhouses, like some farms, are humanely managed. It depends upon the person who is managing them and is in charge of the staff. But many people think that this isn't good enough, and that we need more laws and more supervision to make sure that animals suffer less.

The great debate

More and more people are beginning to worry about intensive farming. They say it is not right that animals are kept without fresh air and exercise in overcrowded conditions so that we can eat cheaper meat.

In the 1920s and 1930s, there was a deep depression in farming. Two-thirds of our food had to be imported. This meant that when the Second World War began in 1939, there was very little to eat.

Over 2.2 million hectares ($5\frac{1}{2}$ million acres) of grassland were hastily ploughed up to grow crops. Women went to work on the land to replace the men who had been called up to fight. The production of food shot up by 70 per cent.

After the war, Britain was deeply in debt. We could not afford to import much food, and the government also wanted to make sure that in future we could feed ourselves in times of war. So farmers were encouraged to produce more and more food, and people came to expect lower and lower prices. This is why intensive farming was developed.

The National Farmers Union points out that animals today are fed much better than they used to be. Pigs, for example, were fed on household scraps and waste food. Now they are given specially balanced diets of wheat, barley and proteins to make them grow faster. They also say that keeping animals in individual pens is better from a welfare point of view, because it stops the weaker ones from being bullied. In intensive systems, temperature and ventilation can be controlled so that the animals are warm and they can easily be inspected for disease.

Those who are in favour of intensive farming say that free-range farming can cause more suffering to the animals. The ground can become wet and muddy, and infested with parasites. Chickens may be eaten by foxes, and sick animals are not so easy to spot.

But is a sow better off in a stall where she cannot even

turn around? Is a hen happier in a battery cage than scratching the ground in the open air? The general public is increasingly asking if we should treat animals like this so that we can have cheap meat. Animal welfare groups are stepping up pressure on the government to change the laws.

It is possible to use the benefits of modern technology without the bad elements. With better diets and controlled environments, our animals could be healthier than ever before. But giving them more space, more freedom and straw bedding for their pens means employing more staff – and those staff must be more skilled. That means that meat would become more expensive.

Yet we've seen how many animals die of disease in intensive systems. This wastage eats into the farmer's profits, and it represents animal suffering. We are also producing far more food in the EEC than we need. Milk quotas mean that many dairy cows have had to be slaughtered, and many hectares of farm land are 'set aside' – that is, not farmed. As time goes by, it is getting harder and harder to make a case for intensive farming.

A better future?

Animal welfare societies such as Compassion in World Farming and the Farm Animal Welfare Council have been calling for changes in the way some of our animals are farmed for a long time. Today many consumers are demanding a better life for these animals too. This creates pressure on the government and the farmers to change things for the better.

There are new scientific developments, such as genetic engineering, which make the future look bleak for our farm animals. But there is some encouraging news too.

- In Denmark and New Zealand, Muslims have voluntarily agreed to eat meat from animals that have been stunned before slaughter.
- A large bacon farm in Yorkshire is asking its producers to change over to outdoor pig-rearing.
- Within the next ten years, cows may be milked by robots. The cow would be able to go into the milking-station whenever she felt like it, instead of waiting to be milked twice a day. This would be more comfortable for her, because her calf would normally suckle her milk six or seven times a day. But there is a drawback to this – robot milking-stations would be best suited to zero-grazing systems where the cow never goes outdoors.
- As more and more people want additive-free meat from free-range animals, some farms are changing to meet the demand. There are now several producers of 'real meat'.
- In the West German state of Hesse and in Switzerland, Holland, Sweden and Tasmania, battery cages are being phased out.
- In Britain, sow stalls are losing popularity. Farmers don't want to invest in them because they think they may be outlawed soon, and because disease spreads quickly among the pigs housed in them. Three of the top pig-breeding companies have bred a pig that is ideally suited to free-range farming.
- Two of Britain's top poultry producers now kill their birds in a more humane way. They have increased the voltage in the water-bath stunner so that the bird is stunned and killed before it leaves the water-bath.
- Compassion in World Farming mounted a campaign to point out the cruelty involved in frogs' legs. As a result,

several leading supermarkets have stopped stocking them. So have many restaurants.

What can *you* do?

- Ask your parents not to buy battery eggs. Egg-boxes that have slogans such as 'Farm fresh', 'Country fresh' or 'Fresh brown eggs' contain eggs from battery hens. The boxes that say 'Free-range', 'Semi-intensive', 'Deep litter' or 'Perchery' are the ones to go for.

- Ask your parents to consider buying meat from free-range animals. You don't have to live in a big town to be able to get it. There are now several farms that will send their meat overnight in vacuum packs to keep it cool. It's more expensive, but it doesn't contain antibiotics or hormones. The Soil Association (address on page 133) will send you a list of farms that meet the required standard.

- Join Farm Animal Rangers (address on page 131). This is the junior branch of Compassion in World Farming. Membership is £2 a year, and for that you get a year's subscription to *Out* magazine, stickers and surprise goodies.

- If you see frogs' legs or pâté de foie gras on sale or offered on a menu, write to Compassion in World Farming (address on page 131) and tell them where you found them. They will contact the shop or restaurant to explain to them the cruelty involved. When they do this, many people refuse to stock them any more.

- Tell your milkman that you would not buy BST milk.

I'd like to express my views on unwanted pets.

Apparently it's not uncommon for pets to be brought into a family household as adorable, desirable gifts. Frequently, during a phase, children will plead for a pet and a hasty decision is reached. But when the enthusiasm wears off, the result is one poor, unwanted pet – and hence the need for the RSPCA and pet homes.

People should realize that pets require a lot of care and attention, and that getting a pet is not a decision that should be taken lightly. I think that we all should bear in mind the frequent abandonment of family pets, and see what practical suggestions we can make to alleviate this worrying problem.

Andrea Barnes, aged 12,
Taunton, Somerset

5

LOOKING AFTER YOUR PET

It's easy to look around and criticize the way that other people treat animals – but can you be confident you're not being cruel to animals yourself?

How often have you seen a grossly overweight dog waddling uncomfortably along? That dog is overfed and doesn't get enough exercise. It doesn't enjoy life as much as a slimmer dog that gallops and romps about and it's likely to die much younger – but its owner probably loves it dearly and would be horrified to be called cruel. And a budgerigar or canary alone in a cage is a common sight, although these are gregarious birds that should never be condemned to loneliness.

Many people are unkind to their pets through ignorance. They don't take the trouble to find out their animals' needs, and sometimes they set their hearts on species that are totally unsuited to their living conditions. Make sure you're not guilty of this. Owning a pet is a responsibility, and it is one to take seriously.

Most families have one sort of pet or another, from cuddly, companionable ones such as dogs to snakes, lizards and stick insects. The important thing is to choose a pet that is right for your particular circumstances.

If you live in a block of council flats, it's probable that pets will be banned. This is to prevent damage and nuisance to neighbours. But don't despair – it's not likely that the

Choosing a suitable pet

council would object to goldfish, which don't bark, scratch at doors or cause a smell!

If you live in a private house or flat, you can have a choice of most types of pet – although the council might draw the line at you keeping a pig or goat in a small back garden in town. But before you rush out and buy a Great Dane, think again. A large dog will need a lot of exercise. Do you have large open spaces near by? And indoors it will take up a lot of room – even a Labrador can clear all the cups off a coffee table with one happy sweep of its tail.

The lifestyle of your family is important too. If your parents work full time and the house is empty all day, it's not fair to keep a dog. It will be very lonely and towards the end of the day it will be in distress, because it will need to relieve itself. Once a dog is house-trained, it will become very upset if it fouls the house. A cat, on the other hand, doesn't need company as much and can go in and out through a cat-flap.

You must also realize that a cat or dog may live for about 15 years, depending on the breed. When they are young, they will need to have someone to keep an eye on them most of the time, and for every day of that 15 years they will need to be fed and looked after. If you're not willing to make a long-term commitment, you'd be better off with a hamster or guinea-pig, which make endearing but less demanding pets. Even so, all animals need regular feeding. If you give them breakfast at eight in the morning before you leave for school, you'll have to stick to the same schedule during holiday-time too.

You should ensure that you have the full agreement of your parents before you set out to get your pet. Feeding a pet costs money, and vets' bills can be large. Your parents will find it hard to love a pet that's putting a severe strain on the family finances, and you'll need their backing.

Once you've decided what type of pet you want, you'll need to consider where to get it. If you're looking for a rabbit, guinea-pig, mouse, hamster or gerbil, you may find someone at school who has bred some extra ones. You may be able to obtain a cage-bird in the same way, or perhaps there may be a breeder who advertises in the local paper. If you have a well-run pet-shop in your town, you can buy from there. Don't get any animal from a badly run pet-shop – it may be diseased.

The best way to get a cat or dog is from a home for stray animals. Sometimes you may even find pedigree kittens or puppies that have been abandoned. These homes will be especially full after Christmas, when unwanted presents have been turned out on the street, and during the summer, when families going on holiday have been unwilling to pay boarding-kennel fees. These animals have had a bad time and deserve a second chance – but if nobody rescues them, they inevitably have to be put down.

If you've got your heart set on a particular breed of cat or dog, it's best to go to a professional breeder. Anyone who has done a good job of breeding healthy and temperamentally sound animals wants to know what sort of home they are going to, and prefers to sell direct.

Whatever sort of pet you have decided on, there will probably be a magazine devoted to it. Any good newsagent will have a list of all the magazines in publication that you will be able to scan for a likely title. You can then ask the newsagent to order a copy for you so that you can look for breeders' advertisements.

Once you have got your pet, it's a good idea to buy a book that deals solely with the care of that particular species. This might be a slim book on hamster-keeping or a thick tome on just one breed of dog! That way you'll get a full range of information on how to give your pet the very best treatment. Another good source of advice is the RSPCA, which for a nominal charge will supply you with helpful leaflets on keeping a variety of pets. In the mean time, here's a brief run-down on what you should expect to provide for the most common types of pet. If you're about to embark on pet-keeping it will help you decide what kind of animal you can manage. If you already have a pet, read on anyway to make sure you are giving it the good care it deserves.

Dogs

Dogs make excellent pets. They're loving, intelligent, responsive and good company. But they do need a certain amount of training and a good deal of exercise, and they shouldn't be left alone at home for long periods.

Dogs come in all shapes and sizes. If you live in the country and your parents are willing to help exercise a dog while you're at school, by all means go for a big one. If you live in town in a little flat, there are plenty of small breeds to choose from.

Temperament is another factor to consider. Some breeds are very placid, while others are more highly strung. If you have small brothers and sisters, choose one of the breeds that are renowned for being good with children, such as a Labrador.

Exercise is vital for a dog, both for its physical condition and its happiness. Large, active breeds need at least 16 kilometres (10 miles) exercise each day. Medium-sized breeds such as Labradors should have a minimum of 9 kilometres (6 miles) and smaller breeds need 3 to 4 kilometres (2 to 3 miles). This doesn't mean that *you* have to cover this distance – your dog will do plenty of leaping and gambolling on his own account, particularly if you throw a ball or he has another dog to play with.

Occasionally you may hear dog-owners say, 'Oh, I can't let him off the lead because he runs away.' This is like saying, 'Oh, my eleven-year-old daughter can't read or write because she never wanted to go to school.' Dogs have to be trained to come when they are called. It's a very simple matter that just requires a little patience, and it is absolutely necessary so that the dog can have his freedom. If the dog isn't trained, then he will have to be kept on a chain in the garden and on a leash for walks – so when he gets the chance, of course he will run away, desperate for some exercise and adventure. So if you're not prepared to take the trouble to learn how to train a dog, don't get one.

You should teach him other things too – not to jump up and leave muddy paw-marks on your clothes is one, and it's useful if he knows the commands 'sit', 'lie down' and 'heel'. Household rules vary – some people won't let their dogs on the furniture while others don't mind at all. That's up to you. The important thing is to train your dog so that he fits in with your life. A well-trained dog is a happy dog, because he knows when he's in the right. Most dogs get upset when they are in trouble, so it's only fair that they should know how to avoid it! And, like well-behaved children, well-behaved dogs are welcomed in more places, so in general they have more fun.

There are plenty of books on how to train dogs. Some of them tend to be a little harsh, so be guided by the temperament of your dog. Some dogs will be quite unabashed by a good smack, while others will quiver miserably for hours at the sound of an angry voice. If yours is the sensitive type, avoid books that recommend sharp yanks on a choke-chain or other physical punishment as forms of discipline. Don't inflict any physical punishment at all unless it's absolutely necessary – if a disapproving voice has the desired effect, it's cruel to go any further.

If you feel you need guidance, you'll probably be able to find a dog-training class in your area. These can be fun, and both you and the dog will enjoy meeting the other classmates. But again, allow for your dog's personality. The instructor should too, but if he or she seems to be making your dog cowed or miserable, don't persist unless the dog is completely out of hand. You can always ask someone you know who has a well-trained dog to lend a hand instead.

Adult dogs should be fed once a day in the evening, although you can offer a few dog-biscuits during the day as a treat. Don't give him chocolate or sweet biscuits – dogs can't have their teeth filled! Don't allow him to beg titbits from the table while you're eating; it can become very irritating, and most visitors will find it disconcerting.

The evening meal should be about two-thirds meat to one-third biscuit. A small dog weighing less than 2.25 kg (5 lb) will need about 150 g (5 oz) of food each day; a dog of about 11 kg (25 lb) needs about 560 g (20 oz); a larger dog of 22 kg (50 lb) will eat about 850 g (30 oz) and one of 45 kg (100 lb) will need about 1.3 kg (3 lb). A puppy will need to be fed several times a day and you should follow the routine he has been accustomed to in his previous home.

A puppy needs special care during his first few days in a new home. He will be feeling frightened, lost and lonely without his mother and brothers and sisters. He'll be in unfamiliar surroundings with people he doesn't know and will be understandably miserable. If you give him plenty of attention and encourage him to play, he'll soon perk up and begin to take his place in the family. But always remember he's just a baby – he may be fun to play with but he'll get tired before you will, so let him have plenty of rest. The same goes for exercise – his little legs will have to work very fast to keep up with yours, so don't attempt long walks until he's older.

All puppies should be vaccinated against distemper, viral hepatitis, kidney leptospirosis and liver leptospirosis. Until his vaccinations are complete, don't allow your puppy on the ground outside your own garden. If you are in any doubt about his welfare, always check with your vet.

Most dogs need to be groomed, but how much of a task

this is depends on the breed. Long-haired breeds obviously need more attention than short-haired ones, and again temperament comes into play – some dogs are naturally fastidious while others will splosh happily through every muddy puddle they can find. Your pet-shop should be able to advise you on the best sort of brush for your dog.

A dog should never, ever be allowed out alone. At best he will foul the pavements and at worst he might cause a serious road accident. The latter can happen even when a dog is out exercising with his owner, so it's wise to take out a third-party liability insurance in case you are sued for damages.

A dog can be the most delightful pet there is – but that's up to you. It's no good leaving a dog alone in a kennel in the garden and then expecting him to be excellent company one day a month when you feel like it. Dogs need attention and loving treatment as part of the family in order to be really responsive and intelligent pets. If you're prepared to put a lot into being a dog-owner, you'll find that your love is returned fourfold.

Cats

Dogs are descended from wolves, which are pack animals. A dog will regard you and the rest of the family as part of his pack and want to integrate fully with you. Cats are a very different matter.

Some cats have the knack of making their owners feel privileged if they deign to notice them at all. A cat is quite capable of accepting dinner and a warm knee to sit on with airy disdain before stalking off into the garden to get on with her own affairs.

This independence is what many people love about cats. It also makes them ideal pets if you don't have enough time to exercise a dog or the house is empty all day.

Yet it doesn't mean you can go off on holiday, leaving a

cat to feed herself on birds and mice. Even if your cat is a good hunter, she has been accustomed to a meal at home every day. If her family disappears, she will be frightened and upset. She may successfully wheedle her way into a more caring home, or she may become one of the many thin strays, which have to survive as best they can.

You may want to have one of the more exotic breeds of cat such as a Burmese or Abyssinian, or perhaps you'd be happy with a common or garden 'moggie'. The latter are easy to find, while a pedigree may cost a good deal of money.

Unless one of your parents is at home all day, you should get a kitten at the beginning of the summer holidays. That way you'll be able to spend plenty of time with it when it's small. It will require a lot of gentle care at first while it settles into its new home, and it will also need to be house-trained.

Like puppies, kittens should be taken to the vet for routine vaccinations against several diseases including feline enteritis and influenza, both of which are killers.

You should provide your cat with a comfortable bed in a quiet position – although you may find that she will decide to sleep somewhere else altogether! Unless her chosen spot is inconvenient, it's best to give in gracefully and let her have her way.

In the wild, cats hunt at night. The domestic cat still has the instinct to do this, but you certainly shouldn't put her out for the night. She may be cold, wet and miserable and she may get run over. Let her go exploring earlier in the evening and then call her in before you go to bed, or else fit a cat-flap so she can come and go as she pleases.

Cats have smaller stomachs than dogs so your pet will need two meals a day, one in the morning and one at night. One should be of meat and the other of biscuit soaked in milk or water. She also needs roughage, so include some vegetables in her food. Cats eat coarse grass which gives them roughage, so if yours lives permanently indoors, you should grow some grass in trays for her. Everyone knows that cats like milk, but they also need fresh water to quench their thirst.

Cats are fastidious and generally won't eat stale food or food served in dirty dishes, so throw away surplus food and wash the dish after every meal. If she is still reluctant to eat, try different diets. If she is off her food for a long period, or

If she is off her food – try different diets

French   Italian   Indian   Chinese

she shows any other symptoms of illness, take her to the vet – although it may be that she has just found someone else to feed her. It's not uncommon for two families to be equally convinced that a cat is theirs because it is eating and sleeping in two homes.

Cats usually take care of their coats themselves, but long-haired breeds may need some grooming to prevent the fur becoming matted. These breeds swallow a lot of fur while they are washing themselves, so it's a good idea to give them liquid paraffin every week as a laxative. This stops fur-balls forming in their stomachs.

Male cats should be neutered when they are between four and five months old. It's a simple operation but a necessary one, because tom-cats don't make good pets. They are often bad-tempered, they fight with other cats, and they mark their territory by spraying it with urine and a strong-smelling secretion. They are also responsible for fathering kittens that are often unwanted and may form part of the colonies of strays.

It's hard to prevent a queen (female cat) from becoming pregnant. She can produce three litters each year, so unless you feel able to find homes for about 24 kittens annually, she should be spayed (neutered). It's a slightly more complicated operation than that needed for a male cat, but it should not pose any problems.

Many people neglect cats because of their apparent independence. Don't take one on lightly – they may require less of your time than a dog, but they still need to be fed and cared for.

Rabbits

Rabbits are very easy to care for, but your choice of breed will be influenced by whether you plan to keep yours in a shed or outdoors. You will need to check how it has been kept in its previous home too – if it has been bred and kept indoors in warm conditions, it will probably get a chill if it is suddenly transferred outside.

The best way to see the different breeds of rabbit is to go to a local show, where there will probably be rabbit classes. You may see just what you want there, and you may be able to approach the owner to ask if he or she has any young to sell. Failing that, you can find out the address of the local rabbit society so that you can inquire there.

Rabbits range in size from Flemish Giants, which can be up to 5 kg (11 lb) in weight, to the Polish and Dutch dwarf breeds, which only reach about 1.3 kg (3 lb). The larger breeds can be quite strong and difficult to handle, so if

rabbit classes...

you're a novice rabbit-keeper, your best bet is to go for a smaller one.

The best way to keep a rabbit is in a hutch with an outdoor run. A medium-sized rabbit will need a hutch measuring at least 120 cm (4 ft) long by 60 cm (2 ft) deep by 60 cm (2 ft) high. If you have more than one rabbit, the hutch will need to be at least 60 cm (2 ft) longer.

The end should be partitioned off to form a sleeping area. Three sides should be solid, and the front should be fitted with 26 mm (1 inch) wire mesh. The roof should be sloping and waterproofed with polythene or roofing-felt, with a generous overhang all round so that the rain can run off. The hutch should stand on legs or bricks to keep it off the wet ground.

It's not likely you'll find a hutch that is big enough in the local pet-shop. If you don't have a parent who is good at DIY, try specialist suppliers or commission a local handyman to make one for you.

Provide plenty of straw, wood shavings, sawdust or newspaper to make a warm, dry bed. If the weather is exceptionally bad, take the hutch into a shed or garage until it improves.

Rabbits need feeding twice a day and this can be done very

cheaply by gathering hedgerow plants and leaves. Don't collect these from the roadside, as they will be contaminated by lead from car exhausts. Don't give too much of any one plant, and avoid frost-damaged or rotting vegetation. And don't feed rabbits rhubarb leaves, potato tops, tomato leaves or the weed coltsfoot; according to the RSPCA, all of these are harmful to them. Your rabbit will also need some cereal such as stale bread, oats or bran and some roots. In cold weather a warm mash of oats, bran, boiled potatoes and vegetables will go down very well.

Myxomatosis, a disease of wild rabbits, is transmitted by fleas, so dust your pet with flea-powder from time to time to be on the safe side. Never put a wild rabbit in with your own pet until you have quarantined it for a month after immediate de-fleaing.

Guinea-pigs

Guinea-pigs aren't as hardy as rabbits, but they still make attractive, easy pets. They will need a hutch similar to a rabbit's, and again it's a good idea to have a sliding door to an outside run so that they can graze and sunbathe. Make sure they have access to shade as well, as they can suffer from sunstroke.

You may keep your guinea-pigs in a hutch indoors and provide them with an outside run that they can use when the weather is good. If so, don't let them suffer extremes of temperature – a very hot day followed by a cool evening may lead to a bout of pneumonia. Take them back indoors before the temperature drops too much.

The best way to buy guinea-pigs is as a pair of the same sex, preferably from the same litter. They will be ready to leave their mother at four weeks old. If no one at your school is able to supply you with some, try to find a local breeder as pet-shop guinea-pigs tend to be of inferior quality.

Guinea-pigs have extremely large appetites and small stomachs, so they need a constant supply of food. This should include cabbage, lettuce, hedgerow plants, grass, leaves, carrots, turnips, swedes, bread, oats and flaked maize. In the summer they will be able to graze all day if they are kept outdoors, but they will still need cereal and hay.

Guinea-pigs will try to fatten themselves up for winter. If yours succeed, cut their food down a little during the winter so that they use up their surplus fat – but don't cut meals out altogether. A hot evening meal will be appreciated during the winter months.

They will also need branches to gnaw at to wear their teeth down. Their teeth continue to grow throughout their life and a diet of soft food will not be enough to keep them in check.

As with rabbits, you should avoid spoiled or frost-damaged vegetation, and the four foods listed on page 105. Make sure there's a constant supply of fresh water – the best way to do this is from a water-bottle with a teat, which you will be able to find in the local pet-shop.

Guinea-pigs come in a range of different colours and, with their playful natures and endearing growls and whistles, make delightful pets.

Mice, hamsters and gerbils

These are all popular as pets and they require very little space, so they are ideal if your home is small.

Mice come in a wide range of attractive colours. The local pet-shop may only have white ones, so you may need to seek out specialist breeders if you want something more unusual.

Take note of how they are kept. If they are living in dirty, overcrowded conditions and they are nervous of being handled, go elsewhere. You can expect young ones to be timid, but adult ones should be happy to sit on the breeder's hand.

Mice are very gregarious animals, so it's kinder to have a colony rather than just one. From your point of view, you'll probably find it fascinating to watch the very complex social structure they will evolve. But don't start off with a large number – they breed so fast that one male and two females can supply you with a colony in little over a month. Mice have a reputation for being smelly and adult males are responsible for much of that. If you have only one male and you clean the cage out regularly, you shouldn't have any problem.

The metal cages you find in pet-shops are too small and rather cold. The best container is a glass aquarium measuring 60 cm (2 ft) in length and 38 cm (15 in) in width and depth. The top should be covered with wire mesh so there is plenty of ventilation, and you should provide plenty of logs, ladders, ropes and exercise wheels. Hay and newspaper will be necessary for bedding and nest-building. Never give them damp soil or peat as damp kills mice.

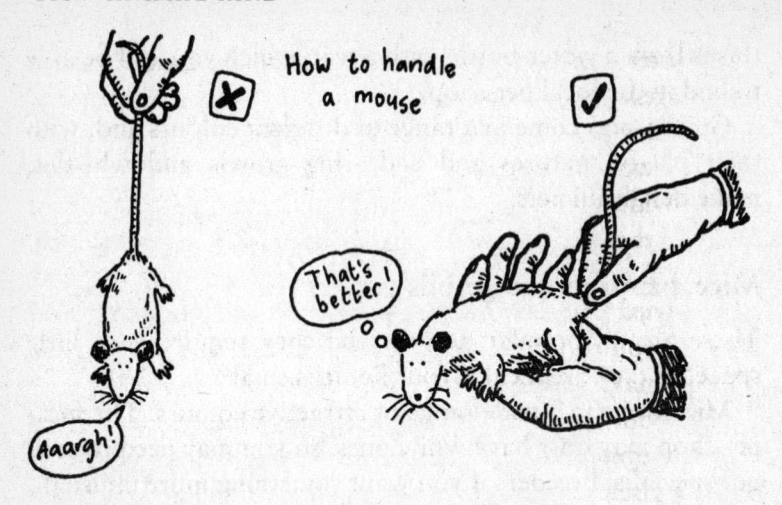

You can buy pelleted mice food, but as mice will eat almost anything it's rather a waste of money. Offer your mice small quantities of bread, cake, cereals, fruit, meat, wheat, barley and maize twice a day and they will be quite happy.

Never pick a mouse up by the end of its tail. Take hold of it by the base of its tail and support it under its body with your other hand. You should handle your mice every day to keep them tame, with the exception of pregnant females.

Female mice shouldn't be allowed to breed until they are three months old. After that, you'll find you have more mice than you know what to do with. It's very unlikely you will be able to find homes for all of them, so you should take them to your vet to be put to sleep.

In contrast to mice, hamsters are very solitary animals. Two adults in a cage will fight to the death, so you will probably want to keep only one, unless you have room for more cages. Hamsters are quite timid and will bite if frightened. Because females are more temperamental, your best bet is to buy a male of about six weeks old. If you handle him gently he will become very friendly, but if you take him by surprise you can still expect a sharp bite.

Hamsters are nocturnal and hibernatory animals, although if they are kept in an even temperature they will stay active all year. In this country they should live indoors. They will gnaw through wooden cages, so again an aquarium tank is ideal, but provide plenty of hardwood branches such as oak or beech so that your pet can keep his front teeth in good shape.

He will need hay or newspaper for bedding, and the tank can be lined with sawdust or dry peat. He will choose a toilet area, so you can put a little container such as a jam-pot lid there to make cleaning out easy.

Feed your hamster once a day, in the evening. He will eat cereals, vegetables, seeds, fruit and nuts, and he will want to make himself a little store of food. Don't stop him doing this as it's one of his basic instincts – just clean it out periodically when it starts to smell and he will start all over again.

Gerbils are also partly nocturnal in the wild, although in captivity this is less noticeable than with hamsters. You can keep several together, but perhaps the happiest arrangement is a male and female pair, as gerbils mate for life.

Their diet is similar to a hamster's and the same kind of aquarium tank will be the best accommodation. Because they are burrowing animals, you will need to fill the tank two-thirds deep with light, loamy soil. It can be difficult to keep the soil from becoming damp and cold, and for this reason some people make tunnels of plaster of paris for their gerbils. As with rabbits and guinea-pigs, don't feed any of these animals rhubarb leaves, potato tops, tomato leaves or coltsfoot.

Tortoises

The only advice on having a tortoise as a pet is – don't. Very few are bred in captivity; the rest are imported from the wild. Traditionally they were taken from the Mediterranean basin, but their numbers became so depleted that this was banned in 1984. Now they are imported from Africa instead.

Between 80 and 90 per cent of the Mediterranean tortoises died in their first year. The African ones are even less suited to this climate, and many of them die in transit too. The best thing is not to be responsible for any part of this cruel trade.

Cage birds

The best birds to go for are canaries and budgerigars, which are commonly bred in captivity. If you have your heart set on something more exotic, do take the trouble to find a bird that has been bred in this country rather than imported from the wild. Thousands of birds are imported into this country each year, often in terrible conditions. Many of them die en route and some species are becoming increasingly rare in the wild because so many have been captured.

Canaries and budgerigars are in any case a good starting-point as they are the easiest birds to care for. They can be kept indoors or out, provided they have access to warm indoor accommodation in bad weather.

If you want a budgerigar that talks, you'll have to keep one solitary bird. If you do this, make sure it has plenty of toys to provide stimulation. It is much kinder, though, to have two so that they can keep each other company. If you only have a standard cage you should have two males, as a male and female pair won't be able to nest and breed properly.

The budgerigar cages sold by pet-shops aren't really ideal as there is nowhere for the bird to hide if it is frightened or to shelter from the sun. They are also very draughty. If you do have this kind of cage, put it in a corner to minimize draughts and add a little security. Much better is a mesh-fronted box, no smaller than $60 \times 45 \times 30$ cm (2 ft $\times$ 18 in $\times$ 12 in). These are easy to make, but you should also be able to obtain one from good pet-shops and specialist suppliers.

If you are going to keep your birds outside, you will be able to provide them with an aviary that really lets them stretch their wings. The birds will be happier and you'll find them more interesting to watch. If your bird lives indoors you may like to let it fly round the room for exercise. Before you release it from the cage, do make sure that doors and windows are closed and that fires and chimneys are guarded.

Budgerigars and canaries are easy to feed. You'll be able to find seed mixtures in all pet-shops and many supermarkets. Supplement this with dandelion leaves or other weeds from the garden and grit made from crushed shell and ground limestone, which you'll be able to obtain from pet-shops.

If you want to try any other type of bird, it's best to consult a specialist breeder and read up about that particular species before you buy.

Fish

An aquarium full of brightly coloured fish is a pleasing addition to any room and it needs very little attention. It's a good idea to buy the largest one you can afford, so that you've got plenty of space for more fish if you become a real enthusiast. Go to a specialist aquarium supplier, who will also be able to equip you properly with heaters, a thermometer and a filtration system and give you advice on how to set it all up.

You'll also need lights, which are usually fitted in the hood of the tank. Don't switch them on or off abruptly so that the fish are subjected to a sudden blaze of light or plunged into darkness. Either fit a dimmer-switch or use them in accordance with natural light to make a gradual change. Never leave them on all night as the fish need a period of darkness.

Put plenty of plants in the aquarium, both to provide hiding-places for the fish and to add oxygen and remove carbon dioxide. Don't allow any of the plants to grow into a mat on the surface or they'll keep light off the smaller plants.

Some types of fish will eat others, so check with your supplier before adding a new species. A new fish should be put in the tank inside the bag you bought it in and only released several hours later when it has adjusted to the new temperature.

There's quite a lot to learn about setting up and stocking an aquarium, so you should read a book on the subject before you start. You may have an aquarist society based near you and, if so, you're bound to find a lot of helpful advice on offer from its members.

Ponies

Buying and keeping a pony is not something to be undertaken lightly. It's no use thinking you can keep one in a shed at the bottom of the garden, or grazing on a patch of waste ground, because you can't.

For a start, being herd animals, ponies are not happy being kept on their own. Shut up in a stable all day without exercise will make them both unhappy and unhealthy; turned out in a field they can get into all kinds of trouble, from injuring themselves on fences to making themselves ill through overeating or eating poisonous plants. Their feet need attention from a blacksmith every 6 weeks or so, and this is expensive. In winter even grass-kept ponies need extra food. Looking after them properly is hard work, takes a lot of time and can cost a great deal of money. If you really want a pony, and are lucky enough to be able to afford one, take the trouble to learn a lot about pony care and riding before you embark on the great adventure.

I enjoy eating meat but I also disagree with killing animals. So to compromise I've become a 'demi-veg'. This means that I eat white meat like fish and chicken but not red meat.

This doesn't mean that I think killing white-meat animals is all right, it's just a way of cutting down on meat-eating. I will probably become fully vegetarian when I am older.

Laura Edwards, aged 13,
Milton Keynes

6

COULD YOU BE A VEGETARIAN?

Until quite recently, the traditional British meal consisted of meat and two veg. There was a small band of vegetarians, but many people thought of them as well-meaning cranks. Red meat was considered to be necessary to make you strong and healthy and, because it was expensive, having meat every day was also a status symbol.

In the last few years things have changed. We've learnt about the cuisines of other countries through travel and television programmes. We take Italian pasta, Indian curries and Chinese sweet-and-sours for granted, so we no longer feel deprived without our meat and two veg. And among our ethnic communities, many people follow vegetarian diets. Consequently, vegetarian meals have appeared on more and more menus in restaurants and in institutions such as hospitals.

But it's not just a broader outlook that's making more and more people turn vegetarian. Some people are doing it because the latest medical advice is that animal fats are bad for us. Others stop eating meat because of the cruelty to animals that's involved.

In Britain alone, more than 500 million chickens, 15.5 million pigs, 29.5 million turkeys, 4 million cattle, 15.5 million sheep and 2.5 million rabbits are killed for food each year. It's hard to visualize those numbers, but try to imagine eating 7 or 8 cattle, 36 sheep, 36 pigs, 750 poultry and several dozen rabbits. That's what the average British person consumes in his or her lifetime.

We don't need meat. It's quite possible to eat a balanced and tasty diet without animal protein and fat. It doesn't take long to learn how to substitute plant protein for meat. And there are plenty of good reasons why we should do it.

What meat-eating means to you

In 1985, Surrey University and the South London Polytechnic did a survey on vegetarianism and health. They found that vegetarians spend less time in hospital and meat-eaters are much more likely to suffer from constipation, appendicitis, gallstones, angina, haemorrhoids, varicose veins and anaemia.

Those aren't the only diseases we get from eating meat and dairy products. The saturated fats contained in animal foods cause heart disease, and low-fibre, high-fat diets have been linked to cancer of the bowel.

In 1983, the National Advisory Committee on Nutrition Education (NACNE) produced a report that called for a change in our eating habits. It recommended cutting our intake of fats, especially animal fats, by one-third. Instead we should eat more fibre from wholefoods, especially fresh fruit and vegetables.

So it's obvious that meat itself isn't good for us. But that's not the only problem.

Each year, the number of reported cases of food poisoning rises. In 1982, there were 14,253 cases. By 1988, the figure was 41,196. That's nearly three times as many. These figures are supplied by the Office of Population Censuses and Surveys, but they are just the tip of the iceberg. It's estimated that for each reported case, somewhere between 10 and 100 cases go unreported. And 80 per cent of them are caused by meat-eating, while most of the remaining 20 per cent are from dairy products.

There are about 900 slaughterhouses in Britain. The EEC will accept exports from only 93 of them. The rest are considered too unhygienic. One common cause of contaminated meat is that knives fouled with animal faeces or urine are used to cut it.

A third reason for caution about eating meat products is

what goes into them. Many of us don't really know what we're eating. If we did, we might hesitate to put it in our mouths.

Many sausages, pies and burgers are made from 'mechanically recovered meat' (MRM for short). This means the pieces of gristle, sinew and fat that are left on bones when the 'good' meat has been cut away. These leftovers are put in large drums containing water and chemicals and revolved at high speed. At the end, a liquid slurry is piped out. The manufacturer can quite legally label his product as containing 80 per cent meat even when it is 80 per cent slurry.

Meat products are often made with parts of the animal you wouldn't normally think of eating, such as lips and cheeks. Until February 1989, many baby foods contained the brains, spinal cord, tonsils and intestines of cattle. Many mothers must have spooned them lovingly into their babies' mouths, happy in the thought that they were giving their little ones a meal high in meat protein. But if they'd actually seen spinal cord, tonsils and intestines lying on a plate, it's not very likely they'd have thought of feeding them to anyone but the cat.

Yet the most worrying thing about eating meat today is the type of food and the amount of drugs the animals are given. In Chapter 4 we looked at what intensive farming means for animals. Now let's see what it means for us, the consumers.

Cattle

We discussed how the milk-producing hormone BST will affect cows and dairy farmers if it is legalized. How will it affect the public?

The answer is that we simply don't know. The drug companies producing BST say that there should be no side-effects, because they cannot find residues in milk – but their research has mainly concentrated on improving milk yields rather than on finding residues. It's not clear whether the hormone would affect the human body or not.

We do know, though, that only healthy animals can produce healthy food. As the cow comes under greater and greater pressure, the quality of her milk will go down. In high-yield milk, important nutritional elements are missing. It's also thought that BST milk will have less protein and more fat in it.

BST is being tested right now throughout the European Community. In Britain, the names of the farms where trials are under way are kept secret. We just don't know if we are drinking BST milk or not. And when the cattle are slaughtered, their meat is sold in the shops as usual. There is no test that can measure the amount of BST in meat.

So far, the firms that are producing BST have invested no less than half a billion dollars in it. This means they are very anxious indeed for it to be legalized, so they are lobbying politicians and spending a lot of money on advertising to persuade us it is safe. They say it is a natural hormone, but it is not – it is chemically different to natural BST. They claim it is 'species specific', meaning that it only affects cows. But it has also been found to affect sheep and even fish. In the 1950s, people with growth problems were injected with natural BST. They didn't grow any bigger, but they suffered fever, nausea and hyperglycaemia (rise in blood sugar).

In the USA, Professor Samuel Epstein of the Department of Environmental and Occupational Medicine at Illinois University has published a report claiming that the drug companies have concealed the facts about what BST will do to the cows' health. He also says that the Food and Drug Administration have not done the right tests to find out what it will do to humans. According to Professor Epstein, it might make baby boys grow breasts and cause breast cancer in adult women.

In the UK, Professor Richard Lacey of the Veterinary Products Committee is concerned that some people might be in danger, because they might not be able to digest BST. He also thinks it might cause us long-term damage because of the change in the nutritional value of the milk.

Some large supermarket chains, including Tesco and Marks & Spencer, say they won't stock BST milk if they are given the choice. But if BST is legalized and there is no law to say that it must be labelled, there won't be any choice.

BSE (bovine spongiform encephalopathy or 'mad cow disease') is even more worrying. It's been affecting herds of cows all over the country, and it has arisen because of the way cattle are fed.

The natural diet of cattle is grass, but today they are given many different things to eat. Calves, for example, are sometimes fattened on Keystart Chocolac – soya, skimmed milk and pigs' blood flavoured with chocolate. Beef cattle are fattened on root crops, barley, fishmeal and dried poultry manure (known as DPM). Dairy cows are fed on high-protein concentrates that often cause them to go lame. And they have also been fed on sheep offal, including brains.

About 5 per cent of British sheep suffer from a disease called scrapie. It makes the tissue of the brain become spongy, and the sheep becomes demented. BSE is remarkably like scrapie, and it's also remarkably like a human disease called Creutzfeldt-Jakob disease.

Creutzfeldt-Jakob disease causes severe senility, and it is very common in parts of the Middle East where people eat a lot of sheep's eyes. So far, the connection between Creutzfeldt-Jakob disease, scrapie and BSE hasn't been proved – but BSE has only appeared since cattle were fed

mad sheep disease

on sheep offal. In zoos, different species of antelope that were fed on sheep offal have died of the same brain disease.

The government has now placed a ban on feeding sheep offal to cattle. Yet the damage has been done. Scientists think that calves inherit BSE from their mothers, and animals can carry the disease for some time before they show any symptoms. We simply don't know how many cows have BSE.

Nor do we know how infectious it is to humans. In the past, offal from cows was used to make hamburgers, pâtés and meat pies. At the time this book was written, the government was saying that only offal and spinal cord could be dangerous – but many scientists disagree. So although cows' offal can no longer be used in meat products, we cannot be sure that beef and milk are completely safe.

There's another problem too. Because the animals don't show symptoms for a long while after they get the disease, farmers sometimes send them to market without even knowing they have it. Then, if the slaughterhouse is unhygienic, blood from infected brains can splash on to other meat.

BSE has come about because of the pressure to turn everything to profit in intensive farming. The desire to find cheap food for the animals is putting our health at risk as well as theirs.

BSE isn't the only example. The chicken litter that is fed to cattle contains feathers and dead birds as well as faeces. In 1989, an outbreak of botulism in cattle was traced to the rotting chickens in their litter feed. Botulism is a form of food poisoning that can kill people.

In spite of these worrying events, the search for profit goes on. Compassion in World Farming reports that at Trawsgoed Experimental Husbandry Farm cows have been fed on silage effluent. When grass is put into 'clamps' and made into silage, a liquid is released that is 200 times more polluting than untreated sewage. In fact, it's a major cause of pollution in our rivers and streams. But as an experiment, it was preserved with formalin and then fed to cows in plastic troughs – because it would have damaged concrete or galvanized ones! The cows didn't show any signs of ill-health from drinking it, which probably means that someone is working out a method of doing this on a larger scale. But could it be good for us to consume an animal that had been drinking a liquid that eats into concrete and metal?

Then there are the drugs the animals are given. A large amount of cattle feed contains antibiotics in low doses. This is because they speed up growth, so the cattle can be sent to market earlier. The animals are also given antibiotics to halt the spread of disease through the herd.

Antibiotics were originally developed to kill bacteria, but if humans or animals are treated with them regularly, the bacteria develop strains that are resistant to them. This means that food poisoning becomes harder and harder to treat. The Center for Disease Control in Georgia, USA, has found that the death-rate from the antibiotic-resistant strain of salmonella is 21 times higher than from the nonresistant salmonella. And as we constantly eat meat with antibiotics in it, we build up our own resistance to their effects.

By eating cattle we can catch their salmonella, campylobacter (the main cause of our 'tummy bugs') and tapeworm. If the time comes when antibiotics have no effect at all against salmonellosis and campylobacter, we shall have only our human folly to blame.

Pigs

Before they are sent to market at 24 weeks old, pigs are fed on growth-boosting antibiotics. But these aren't enough to prevent the disease that sweeps through factory-farmed animals. When a vet prescribes further antibiotics to cure illness, the farmer is supposed to keep the pig back from slaughter for ten days, so that there is no trace of the drug left in the meat.

Yet this doesn't happen. In 1985, more than a quarter of the pigs' kidneys tested by the Ministry of Agriculture contained residues of sulphadimidine. They were at concentrations 11 times higher than government limits.

Sulphadimidine is the drug most misused in intensive farming. Many pigs are diseased and do need treating. But it's in the farmer's interest to give it to healthy animals too, so that they don't become ill and delay going to market. Also, many vets dispense drugs. This means that the more drugs they prescribe, the more money they make. So many vets and farmers get round the rules on prescribing drugs by saying that the herds are 'in danger of getting ill'.

In the USA, sulphadimidine is suspected of causing cancer. The Food and Drug Administration is planning to ban it. But in the UK, the Ministry of Agriculture considers it to be safe. This is because we have different ways of interpreting animal experiments.

Pigs are fed on sheep offal, as cows were before BSE was linked to scrapie. The Ministry of Agriculture says that they don't live long enough to develop brain disease. But because animals can have the virus for some time before they show any symptoms, many people aren't reassured by this.

Sheep

Because sheep aren't intensively farmed as yet, they still eat a natural diet. We don't eat their brains in the UK because they are small and difficult to remove from the skull, but we do eat other sheep offal such as liver and kidneys.

This might seem illogical when cattle offal is now banned from meat products in case BSE is transmitted to humans – and cows are believed to have developed BSE from eating sheep with scrapie. But the Ministry of Agriculture says that scrapie has been known for over 200 years and there has never been a link established with Creutzfeldt-Jakob disease. Although BSE and scrapie are linked, it says that BSE is a new disease and so it is treating it with extra caution.

In spite of the fact that sheep are extensively farmed, we can still catch food poisoning from eating them, and by handling raw or undercooked sheep meat we can get toxoplasmosis. This can cause blindness, brain damage or death to unborn babies.

Poultry

Studies by the Public Health Laboratory Service show that at least 6 out of 10 chickens sold in the shops are infected with salmonella. The infection is severe enough to give people food poisoning unless the birds are thoroughly cooked. Listeria, another form of food poisoning, is found in 30 per cent of the samples.

One reason why so many of the birds have salmonella is that they are fed on ground-up dead chickens, many of which are diseased, and chicken litter. This causes a constant cycle of infection.

The eggs that come from chickens with salmonella are also infected. The Ministry of Agriculture has begun to destroy egg-laying flocks with salmonella. As yet, it has done nothing about the broiler flocks that we eat.

Like chickens, turkeys are treated with antibiotics for several diseases. The Ministry of Agriculture claims that antibiotics are not used to make them grow faster. Yet the Handbook of Medicinal Feed Additives 1989–90 lists 18 different growth-promoting antibiotics suitable for turkeys. And in 1989, scientists found 13 drug-resistant strains of salmonella in the turkeys they tested.

What meat-eating means to the world

To feed the millions of animals that we eat, we must grow millions of tons of crops. At present, about 90 per cent of Britain's farmland is used for grazing or for growing animal feed.

It's a very inefficient way of feeding ourselves. If we were to put the plants straight into our mouths instead of processing them into animal protein, we could manage on only about 25 per cent of the land that is now farmed.

About 40 per cent of the world's cereal harvest goes to feed livestock. Some of that harvest is exported from countries with famine areas. For example, in 1984 the UK spent £1.5 million importing animal feed from Ethiopia. Each year Europe imports 14 million tonnes of the Third World's harvest.

In the West, we can allow ourselves the luxury of meat-eating – and luxury it must indeed seem to the people of the

Third World. For it takes 45 kg (100 lb) of feed to produce 13.5 kg (30 lb) of eggs. A ton of beef requires 7 tons of cereal. And a dairy cow drinks 32 litres (20 gallons) of water each day.

Imagine five football pitches. That amount of land will feed 61 people if it's used for growing soya. If it's planted with wheat, it will feed 24 people. If maize is grown, it will support 10 people. And if it's used for rearing cattle, it will feed only 2 people.

It's just not possible for all the people in the world to eat a Western diet – there isn't enough land to go round. As it is, the environment is under pressure just to supply the West with its meat. Rain forest in South America is cleared to provide grazing for cattle that will end up as beefburgers. The manure from the cattle gives off methane gas, which contributes to the greenhouse effect. And back here in England, our wildlife dwindles because hedges have been rooted out, marshes drained and ponds filled in to provide more land for growing grain.

What's the verdict?

What we eat is our own decision. Some people are vegan, which means they don't eat any animal products at all. Some are vegetarian – they don't eat meat, but they do eat dairy products and sometimes fish. Other people choose not to eat any factory-farmed food.

Your decision will be influenced by your parents. They may not want one vegetarian in the family. They may feel that you'd grow out of it anyway, or they may back you up enthusiastically. A lot may depend on the family finances – free-range animals that grow without the aid of drugs make expensive meat, whereas a vegetarian diet is generally cheaper than one that includes any meat at all.

If you do decide to become a vegetarian, you'll be part of a growing trend. Vegetarian pop stars include Madonna, Chrissie Hynde, Morrissey, Yazz and Michael Jackson. And the famous Oxo family of the television commercials is now cooking with a vegetable stock-cube instead of a beef one.

What can *you* do?

- Join the Vegetarian Society (address on page 133). They'll send you *Greenscene*, their magazine for young vegetarians, and plenty of helpful leaflets.

- If you decide to become a vegan, contact the Vegan Society (address on page 133). You'll need advice on how to get all the vitamins you require.

- Campaign for vegetarian meals in your school. The Vegetarian Society will send you advice, posters and petition forms. You don't have to be a vegetarian yourself to want other people to have the choice.

- Try some vegetarian meals. There are plenty of excellent cookery books in bookshops and libraries.

USEFUL ADDRESSES

ANIMAL AID YOUTH GROUP
7 Castle Street
Tonbridge
Kent TN 1DL

THE BADGER TRUST
PO Box 631
Bristol
BS99 1UD

BRITISH UNION FOR THE ABOLITION OF VIVISECTION (BUAV)
16a Crane Grove
Islington
London N7 8LB

COMPASSION IN WORLD FARMING
20 Lavant Street
Petersfield
Hampshire
GU32 3EW

FARM ANIMAL RANGERS
20 Lavant Street
Petersfield
Hampshire
GU32 3EW

GREENPEACE
30–31 Islington Green
London N1 8BR

LEAGUE AGAINST CRUEL SPORTS
Sparling House
83–87 Union Street
London SE1 1SG

LORD DOWDING FUND FOR HUMANE RESEARCH
51 Harley Street
London W1 1DD

LYNX
PO Box 509
Dunmow
Essex
CM6 1UH

NATIONAL ANTI-VIVISECTION SOCIETY (NAVS)
51 Harley Street
London W1 1DD

NATIONAL COUNCIL FOR CIVIL LIBERTIES
21 Tabard Street
London SE1 4LA

ROYAL SOCIETY FOR THE PREVENTION OF CRUELTY TO ANIMALS (RSPCA)
Causeway
Horsham
Sussex
RH12 1HG

SOIL ASSOCIATION
86 Colston Street
Bristol
BS1 5BB

THE VEGAN SOCIETY
33–35 George Street
Oxford
OX1 2AY

THE VEGETARIAN SOCIETY
Parkdale
Dunham Road
Altrincham
Cheshire
WA14 4QG

WHALE AND DOLPHIN CONSERVATION SOCIETY
20 West Lea Road
Bath
Avon
BA1 3RL

WORLD WIDE FUND FOR NATURE
Panda House
Godalming
Surrey
GU7 1XR

ZOO CHECK CHARITABLE TRUST
Cherry Tree Cottage
Coldharbour
Dorking
Surrey
RH5 6HA

INDEX

Animal Aid Youth Group, 58, 131
animal testing
  for cosmetics, 51–2
  for drugs, 44–9
animal welfare groups
  campaigns against animal testing, 43, 52
  and export of animals for slaughter, 86
  and intensive farming, 88
Animals (Scientific Procedures) Act, 1986, 47, 48
antibiotics, 64, 75, 124, 127
Arctic foxes, 55–6
Argentina, dissection banned in, 50–51
Australia
  cattle in, 67
  sheep in, 79

badger-baiting, 31–2
Badger Trust, 131
Badgers Act, 1973, 32
balance of nature, 15–16
Bangladesh, frog trade in, 79, 80
bears, in circuses, 12
beavers, 53
big cats
  in circuses, 13
  fur trade and, 3, 55
birds
  shooting of, 36–8
  used in testing, 44
  see also cage birds
black rhino, 14
botulism, 124
Brazil, frog farms in, 80
British Field Sports Society, 22, 24
British Union for the Abolition of Vivisection (BUAV), 46, 49, 131
British Veterinary Association, 83, 84
BSE (bovine spongiform encephalopathy), 122–4, 126

BST (bovine somatotropin), 65–6, 120–22
budgerigars, 110–11
bullfighting, 34–6

cage birds, 110–11
cages, animals in, 12, 13, 15
calves, 68–9
Canada, fur trade in, 53–5
canaries, 110–11
cancer, 50
cats, 94, 100–3
   used in testing, 44, 45
cattle, 64–9, 117, 122, 124
cereal harvests, 127–8
chemicals, 11
   use of, in agriculture, 3
chickens, 75–6, 117
chimpanzees, used in testing, 44
circus animals, 12–13
cockfighting, 19
Compassion in World Farming, 73–4, 81, 88, 124, 131
cosmetics, animal testing and, 43, 51–2
coyotes, trapping of, 53
Creutzfeldt-Jakob disease, 122, 126

dairy cows, 64–6, 122
deer, 27, 81–2
deer-hunting, 25–7

diseases, from eating meat, 118–19
dissection in school syllabuses, 50–51
dog-fighting, 32–4
dogs, 94, 96–100
   used in testing, 44, 45
dolphins, 10
drag-hunting, 28
drugs
   animal testing and, 45, 46, 49–50
   given to animals, 124, 125

elephants, viii, 3, 4–6
   in circuses, 13
endangered species, 3–4
environmental damage, by killing frogs, 80
environmental pollutants, testing for, 47
European Convention for Protection of Animals Kept for Farming Purposes, 73
experiments on animals, 44–52
export
   of animals for slaughter, 85–6
   of laboratory animals, 48–9
   of veal calves, 68, 69

INDEX

Farm Animal Rangers, 90, 131
Farm Animal Welfare Council, 56, 84, 88
farmers, and foxes, 21
farming, intensive methods of, 63–90
Faroe Islands, whale killing in, 10–11
fish, aquarium, 111–13
food-poisoning, 119, 126
fox-hunting, 20–24
foxes, 20–22
    fur trade and, 53, 56
France
    battery hens in, 73
    bullfighting in, 35–6
    export of animals to, 85
    forcefeeding of geese in, 77–8
free-range farming, 87–8
frogs, 44, 50, 79–80
Fur Breeders Association, 56
fur farms, 55–6
Fur Institute of Canada, 53, 54
fur trade, 52–7

game birds, 36–7
geese, 77–8
genetic engineering, 65, 66, 88
Geoffroy's cat, 55
gerbils, 50, 109

Greenpeace, 55, 132
grouse shooting, 36
guinea-pigs, 105–7

habitats, loss of, 5, 7–8
hamsters, 50, 108–9
hare-coursing, 28–9
hare-hunting, 28
hares, 28–30
heart disease, 49–50
hens, 72–6
Hong Kong, ivory trade in, 6
hormones, for farm animals, 66, 78
horse-racing, 38
horses, used in bullfighting, 35
hunting, 20–31

India, frog trade in, 80
Indonesia, frog trade in, 79, 80
intensive farming, 64, 86–8
    of cattle, 64–9, 123–4
    of pigs, 70–71, 125
    of poultry, 71–8
International Convention for the Regulation of Whaling, 9
International Whaling Commission, 9, 10
ivory trade, 4, 5–6

Japan
  ban on ivory trading, 6
  whaling in, 9
Jews, and animal
  slaughtering laws, 83

Kenya, black rhino in, 14

League Against Cruel
  Sports, 20, 22, 38–9,
  132
legislation
  on animal
    experimentation, 47, 48
  to protect wildlife, 32, 38,
    72, 81
  on slaughterhouses, 82,
    86
London Zoo, 13–14
Lord Dowding Fund for
  Humane Research, 132
lynx, trapping of, 53, 55
Lynx (anti-fur organization),
  53, 55 132

meat-eating, 118–28
mice, 50, 107–8
  used in testing, 44, 45
milk, 65–6, 88
  BST and, 121–2
mink, fur trade and, 53, 56
mink-hunting, 30–31
Muslims, and animal
  slaughtering laws, 83, 89

National Anti-Vivisection
  Society (NAVS), 59, 132
National Council for Civil
  Liberties, 132
National Farmers Union, 73,
  87
Norway, whaling in, 9

ocelot, trapping of, 55
opinion polls
  on deer-hunting, 27
  on fox-hunting, 21, 24
  on trapping for fur, 58
otter-hunting, 30
otters, 30, 31, 53

pandas, 7–8
parrots, 3–4
partridges, 37
pesticides, 29
pets, 93–113
pheasants, 36, 37
pigeons, 37
pigs, 70–71, 89, 117, 125–6
polar bears, 15
pollution, 3, 11, 124
  from broiler sites, 76
ponies, 113
Portugal, bullfighting in, 36,
  38
poultry, 71–8
  slaughter of, 84, 89
Protection of Animals Act,
  1911, 81

Protection of Birds Act, 1954, 72
public opinion, ix, 58

rabbits, 103–5, 117
　used in testing, 44, 51
rats
　dissection of, 50
　used in testing, 44, 45
robot milking-stations, 89
rooks, 37
Royal Society for the Prevention of Cruelty to Animals (RSPCA), 12, 34, 96, 132
　on fox-hunting, 20, 22
　on vivisection, 43, 49

salmonella, 124–5, 126–7
Scandinavia
　ban on ritual slaughter in, 83
　fur farms in, 56
scrapie, 122, 126
sheep, 78–9, 117, 122, 126
　export of, 85
slaughterhouses, 82–6, 119
　for battery hens, 73
snares, 56
Soil Association, 133
Spain
　bullfighting in, 34, 35
　slaughterhouses in, 85
sport, animals as, 19–39

sulphadimidine, 125
Sweden
　animal experimentation in, 49
　battery hens in, 89
Switzerland
　ban on ritual slaughter in, 83
　battery hens in, 89

Taiwan, frog farms in, 80
television, wildlife on, 12
'terrier men', 22, 23
tigers, in circuses, 13
tortoises, 109–10
tradition, in sport, 19, 28, 37, 38
trapping animals, for fur trade, 53–5
turkeys, 77, 117, 127

USA
　animal experimentation in, 47–8
　BST in, 121–2
　cattle in, 66, 67
　fur trade in, 53
USSR
　fur trade in, 53
　whaling in, 9

vaccination
　drugs and, 46
　for pets, 99, 101
veal calves, 68–9

Vegan Society, 133
Vegetarian Society, 130, 133
vegetarianism, 117–18, 129–30
venison, 80–81
vets, farm animals and, 63–4
vivisection, 43, 44–50

whales, 8–11
wild animals, imported to zoos, 14–15

wildfowl, 37
wildlife, 3–16
wolves, trapping of, 53
World Wide Fund for Nature, 7, 133

zero-grazing systems, 64, 89
Zoo Check, 15, 16, 133
zoos, 13–15

Also in Puffin

ENVIRONMENTALLY YOURS
Early Times

What is the greenhouse effect? Why is the Earth getting warmer? Who is responsible for the destruction of the countryside? Where can you get advice on recycling? When will the Earth's resources run out? The answers to all these questions and many more are given in this forthright and informative book. Topics such as transport, industry, agriculture, population and energy are covered as well as lists of 'green' organizations and useful addresses.

THE ANIMAL QUIZ BOOK
Sally Kilroy

Why do crocodiles swallow stones? Which bird migrates the furthest? Can kangaroos swim? With over a million species, the animal kingdom provides a limitless source of fascinating questions. In this book Sally Kilroy has assembled a feast for enquiring minds – from domestic animals to dinosaurs, fish to footprints, reptiles to record breakers. Discover where creatures live, how they adapt to their conditions, the way they treat each other, the dangers they face – you'll be surprised how much you didn't know.

DEAR JO
Early Times

Have *you* ever had a real problem like falling out with your best friend; not being able to read properly because of dyslexia; feeling lonely and unloved because your parents have separated; being hooked on *Neighbours* and not able to think of anything else?

Well, maybe you're not alone! Lots of others feel the same way and many of them ask for help by writing to advice columnists like Jo in *Early Times*. Just telling someone else about your problems can make things better, and getting a helpful, kind and often funny letter back can soon put a smile back on the glummest of faces!

In this book you'll find the answers to lots of problems you may have had, or are likely to have while you're growing up. Some are serious, some more light-hearted – so have a good read, a bit of a giggle and *do* stop worrying!

THE PUFFIN BOOK OF HANDWRITING
Tom Gourdie

How to write well with everyday materials. Write an alphabet in a tree of hearts, fill in word puzzles, trace letters, draw line patterns, have fun and acquire an elegant style of handwriting. These exercises have been devised to help you learn how to write beautifully.

THE PUFFIN BOOK OF DANCE
Craig Dodd

From ballet to Broadway, this book is packed with fascinating information for all young dance fans. From the evolution of dance in all its forms to dance classes, schools and techniques, the life of professional dancers, how dances are made and much more besides, this book captures the glamour and excitement of this spectacular art form.

THE EARLY TIMES BOOK OF CROSSWORDS

There are TV and radio puzzles, Hallowe'en puzzles, skeleton puzzles, science puzzles as well as straightforward crossword puzzles to keep you going for hours, days, weeks, months – in fact, as long as your brain can stand it. Whether you're a beginner or an addict, this book of crosswords from *Early Times* will make you think and keep you puzzling.

GOING IT ALONE
Jody Tresidder

Ever thought it's time to leave home? Ever thought you'd like a flat of your own? And when the moment comes to choose, are you going to stick with school or college or go for a real job? Or could you go off abroad? Or even set up a company of your own? Here at last are the answers for every teenager who feels it's time they took control of their own lives.

WHOSE SIDE ARE YOU ON?
Martyn Forrester

Smoking – nuclear weapons – bullfighting – blood sports – all issues of tremendous importance, where you need to know the facts before you form your own opinions. This book has all the arguments in one book, presented by the people who really know what they are talking about: the supporters and opposers themselves.

GIRLS ARE POWERFUL
ed. Susan Hemmings

How does being a girl or a young woman affect the way people treat you? The way you are allowed to look and dress? Your friendships? And how are all these experiences affected by your class and race? *Girls are Powerful* looks at all these issues and more. But it's not a book 'just' for girls. The pieces in this collection are written by young women aged from seven to twenty-two, but they contain ideas which will open up discussions between women of all ages – perhaps for the first time.

Non-fiction from Dick King-Smith

COUNTRY WATCH

Animal watching can be fascinating and fun – if you know what to look out for and how best to observe it. There are so many different kinds of animals to see in the British countryside and it's not only the unusual ones that are interesting. *Country Watch* is full of surprising facts (did you know that the tiny mole can burrow its way through thirty pounds of earth in an hour?) and Dick King-Smith has lots of marvellous stories to tell about his own encounters with animals over the years.

TOWN WATCH

It's surprising how many wild animals there are to be seen in towns today. *Town Watch* is crammed with information about the many mammals, birds, insects and reptiles that live within the bounds of our towns and cities. Did you know that the cheeky house-sparrow is really one of the tough guys of the bird world, roaming the city in gangster-style mobs? From rubbish-tip pests like rats and cockroaches to protected species such as owls and bats, this book has a wealth of information and stories about urban wildlife.

WATER WATCH

If you look at a map of the world, you'll see that most of its surface is sea. We are surrounded by water – all around us there are lakes, ponds, rivers and streams – not to mention man-made waterways like canals. On holiday at the seaside you can enjoy identifying all the different kinds of gull, or if you're near a rocky coastline you might even see a seal! And there are all sorts of water birds – some with very unusual habits – living near lakes and marshes. You'd have to be lucky to spot an otter but if you're patient and observant, there are some fascinating animals to be spotted in and around a garden or village pond.

PUFFIN BOOK OF ROYAL LONDON
Scoular Anderson

Nowadays the word palace can mean any grand building, but this is a book about a very special group of palaces – the Royal Palaces of London – where the kings and queens of Britain lived and where the present Queen lives today.

Find out which were the favourite palaces and which one had a nasty pong; how the royals got about before cars, trains and buses; why they were sometimes sentenced to death and executed at the Tower; what they did for entertainment and what they ate at the royal banquets! Banquets, beefeaters and beheadings abound in this hilarious guide to Royal London.

PETS FOR KEEPS
Dick King Smith

Keeping a pet can be fascinating and great fun, but it is important to choose the right pet: one that will fit in with your family and surroundings, one that you can afford to keep. This book is packed with useful information about budgies, hamsters, cats, guinea-pigs, mice rabbits, gerbils, canaries, bantams, rats, goldfish and dogs – Dick King-Smith's expert advice and amusing stories about some of the pets he has known and loved make this a practical and entertaining book.

ATTACKS OF OPINION
Terry Jones

Whether you agree or disagree with them, you can't ignore Terry Jones's satirical articles on topical and controversial issues, written in his own ironical, biting style, with brilliant cartoons by Gerald Scarfe.